HADLEY FREEMAN has been a columnist and staff writer for the *Guardian* since 2000, where she writes the popular 'Ask Hadley' column. She also contributes to US *Vogue*. She lives in London.

From the reviews of *Be Awesome*:

'Freeman manages to be both scathing and serious about being awesome in a way no British writer could … The writing is fresh, original. It is tempting to gorge on this collection at breakneck speed. But it works better as a series of witty polemics on women's place in society'
Observer

'Freeman writes with real passion and cold fury … and she writes warmly and kindly about dating, sex and how to cope when all your friends suddenly disappear into the baby-making void … It's good to know you have someone that fearless, funny and – yes – awesome in your corner'
Stylist

'Reading this memoir-cum-conversation is like sitting in a pub with a group of girlfriends, setting the world to rights'
Sunday Times

'Though angry she is rueful, though witty she admits her complicity. Fiercely she recommends books, films, female role models, sexual attitudes and nutritional advice'
The Times

By the same author

The Meaning of Sunglasses

BE
AWESOME

MODERN LIFE FOR MODERN LADIES

Hadley Freeman

FOURTH ESTATE • *London*

Fourth Estate
An imprint of HarperCollins*Publishers*
77–85 Fulham Palace Road
Hammersmith, London W6 8JB
www.4thestate.co.uk

This Fourth Estate paperback edition published 2014

1

First published in Great Britain by Fourth Estate in 2013

Copyright © Hadley Freeman 2013

Hadley Freeman asserts the moral right to be
identified as the author of this work

A catalogue record for this book is
available from the British Library

ISBN 978-0-00-748570-3

'The Drugs Don't Work' words and music by Richard Ashcroft © 1996,
reproduced by permission of EMI Virgin Music Ltd, London W1 9LD

Set in Minion with Stempel Schneidler display by
G&M Designs Limited, Raunds, Northamptonshire
Printed and bound in Great Britain by
Clays Ltd, St Ives plc

MIX
Paper from
responsible sources
FSC C007454

FSC™ is a non-profit international organisation established to promote
the responsible management of the world's forests. Products carrying the
FSC label are independently certified to assure consumers that they come
from forests that are managed to meet the social, economic and
ecological needs of present and future generations,
and other controlled sources.

Find out more about HarperCollins and the environment at
www.harpercollins.co.uk/green

For my awesome sister Nell

'Above all, be the heroine of your life, not the victim' **Nora Ephron**

'Girls, if boys say something that's not funny, you don't have to laugh' **Amy Poehler, American actress and comedian**

'The world is full of guys. Be a man! Don't be a guy' *Say Anything*

Contents

Life is pain … but it doesn't have to be painful, aka the introduction

'Life is pain, highness. Anyone who says differently is selling something.'

Thus spake the Dread Pirate Roberts/Wesley to Buttercup in the glorious 1987 movie, *The Princess Bride*. Aside from learning that one should 'never go in against a Sicilian when death is on the line', this is probably the most valuable lesson that wise film taught me. But, contrary to what the Dread Pirate Roberts/Wesley* appears to advise in this scene, I have never believed that one should just accept it.

The Nietzschean pirate was not wrong. Life is definitely pain: the *Daily Mail* exists; there are still people in the world who believe that banning abortion will lead to happy families as opposed to mutilated women; every straight man I've ever met prefers boring Audrey Hepburn in *Breakfast at Tiffany's* to glorious Katharine Hepburn in *The Philadelphia*

---

* Look, just see the movie, OK? Not only will the whole 'Dread Pirate Roberts/Wesley' thing make sense but your life will be immeasurably improved.

*Story** and, call me a crazy idealist, but I'd have thought that by the twenty-first century any movie that suggests the only happy ending for a woman is marriage would be deemed as unacceptable as any movie that suggests the only jobs available to black people are maids, drug dealers, sassy best friends or Nelson Mandela. Oh. Wait a minute.

Then there are the pains that come from within and, going purely from my own experiences and observations, women are particularly enthusiastic about inflicting these on themselves, almost as much as some of the aforementioned exterior agencies are about inflicting them on them, and it is entirely possible that the two sides to this equation are not unrelated, even an ever-interlooping system. After all, bullies look for susceptible targets.

This is not to suggest that women are delicate victims who need protection, or that feminism treats them as if they are, or whatever nonsense some folk come out with to justify not confronting such things: 'Show me a smart, competent young professional woman who is utterly derailed by … an inappropriate comment about her appearance and I will show you a rare spotted owl,' one journalist wrote in an editorial in the *New York Times*[2] in 2011, suggesting that secretly women love to be reduced to their physical appearance and only pretend they don't because they think

---

* A world in which any man prefers a limpid-eyed actress playing a jewellery-obsessed hooker in the dishonest (Truman Capote's alter ego is, for some reason, rendered straight) and racist (Mickey Rooney plays a Japanese man – let us speak no more of it) to a flashing-eyed woman imperiously entrancing Jimmy Stewart and Cary Grant is, by definition, disappointing.

[2] 'In Favour of Dirty Jokes and Risqué Remarks', Katie Roiphe, *New York Times*, 12 November 2011.

to do otherwise would be a betrayal of the Sistahz and their 'Orwellian' attitudes to sexual harassment. But then this journalist also seems to think that a woman's age ('young') and employment status ('professional') are in any way relevant to her credibility as a sensible person and, rather more jarringly, suggests that only weak women can't handle harassment (or worse), thus putting the focus and blame on the women's reactions rather than the men's actions (an all too common tack in a variety of contexts), so perhaps we need not waste any more of our time on this theory. Although I can't help but regret not getting to see that owl. I do like an owl.

It's hard to be awesome in an occasionally lame world. That so many bizarrely retrograde clichés and expectations still dominate so much of society and pop culture is depressing enough; the number of people who perpetuate them, internalise them and even enact them because, I guess, it's easier to do this than to come up with one's own ideas, one's own arguments, one's own life, can feel downright deadening on a person's soul.

As a woman who works in the media and watches a lot of movies, I, inevitably, notice this in particular in regard to the depiction of women in the media and movies. This, I guess, is because feminism has arrived at something of an awkward place in that while equal rights (if not equal pay) are, at the very least, expected, anachronistic expectations and depictions of women remain. But to be honest, the fact that we're even talking about feminism or, specifically, the definition thereof is depressing because it seems spectacularly lame to have to stroke one's chin about what gender equality means. I have yet to see a single article asking, say, 'Are Civil Rights Dead?' or 'Is the Fight Against Racism Relevant to

Twenty-First-Century Fiction?', to paraphrase two recent chin-strokey articles about feminism, neither of which, incidentally, came from the strawmen of daft right-wing tabloids but two ostensibly liberal and ostensibly respected British publications.* It never ceases to amaze me how much of a meal people still make about the definition of gender equality. I'd have thought that the clue was in the name, but then I always was very literal-minded.

The ubiquitous clichés about life in general, and what one needs to do in order for it to be a fulfilling one – again, going by my personal experience – tend to impinge on one's subconscious and fester during one's twenties and thirties, bringing with them the four horsemen of the apocalypse: self-doubt, panic, insecurity and credulity. One knows when these have arrived because one finds oneself reading the *Daily Mail* website, Mail Online, and giving a toss about it.

But contrary to what a certain pirate claimed, one does not have to accept this, or insist that one is unaffected by them because to do otherwise would be a cop-out of some sort, and I swear I'm not trying to sell you anything. Well, other than this book and, seeing as you're on the fourth page I'm assuming you've already bought it.

Instead, one needs to confront these stereotypes and assumptions and then one can see their stupidity clearly. Wait a minute, 'one'? Who talks like that, other than David Starkey? As I am (spoiler alert) not David Starkey, I shall, briefly, stop hiding behind the presumptuous 'you' and coy 'one' – 'I'. Ta da! There is not a single word in this book that is not directed at myself. All the lessons in this book are lessons

---

* 'Is Feminism Dead?', *New Statesman*, 27 November 2007 and 'Is Feminism Relevant to 21st-Century Fiction', *Independent*, 13 May 2011.

I learned by falling flat on my Semitic-nosed face. This has been the way of my whole career. In the daylight hours – as opposed to the evening ones in which the majority of this book was written – I pretend to be a newspaper columnist and a fashion writer, and at a conservative estimate, at least 70 per cent of my fashion articles have been written when I've been wearing, at best, vaguely coordinated pyjamas, by which I mean a 'Vote Obama 2008!' T-shirt (customised with tea and Marmite stains), leggings and Ugg boots. It's how Anna Wintour edits *Vogue*, you know. Those who cannot do, teach; those who cannot teach, teach gym; those who cannot teach gym, write bossy essays on the subjects at which they so consistently fail.

Few can understand why they believe or are doing something in the moment of believing or doing. That generally comes in the sentimentalised light of retrospect or – more brutally if more usefully – if someone else shines a shaming spotlight on it at the time. This brings me to the tale of what happened when Erinsborough withered under the pitiless gaze of Gallic scorn.

One afternoon when I was thirteen I signed up for the French exchange programme at my school, presumably having hit my head very hard in PE that morning. This brief act of insanity resulted in some random French kid coming to stay with me for two weeks and then I went to stay with her for another two weeks. We were paired together purely by our corresponding ages and, I strongly suspect, our shared religion, or maybe it was just a coincidence that our schools just happened to put together the only two Jewish girls in the programme. Contrary to what our teachers perhaps envisioned, this French girl, who I will call Fifi for no defensible reason, and I did not do renditions of dance routines from *Fiddler on the Roof* and debate the finer points of the Talmud while sitting round a campfire made of Chanukah candles. We hated one another as only two teenagers who don't speak one another's language and are forced to spend a solid month with one another can.

Yet while I returned from the experience with no greater understanding of the perfect and imperfect tenses than I had at the start, Fifi did teach me something else that had nothing to do with linguistics. On her first day, I brought Fifi to school with me and, afterwards, being an extremely cool and cutting-edge teenager, brought her directly home afterwards so as not to miss even the opening notes of the theme song for the essential daily viewing of *Neighbours* and *Home and Away*. As I sat there on the sofa, bowl of grated cheese in my lap ('*L'après école repas du choix*,' I explained to a nauseated-looking Fifi), mouth possibly a little slack with excitement at the gripping storylines involving someone not paying for a caravan in Summer Bay, and Madge and Harold going on a hot date in Lou's Place, I felt what would soon be a familiar sensation: Fifi's disapproving eyes upon my face.

'What is this?' she asked in an accent I'm just about resisting rendering phonetically.

'Oh, they two are TV movies in Australia,' is what I said in French. Speaking one another's language badly was how Fifi and I communicated for the whole of the month, meaning that we were not only never speaking the same language, we were hardly ever speaking any language at all.

'They are good?'

'They super cool.'

'They do not please me.'

'OK. They please me.'

'What stories they tell, please?'

'Much stories. This one, two old people eat dinner in an expensive restaurant. Other, a person did not pay for a car.'

'That sound not interesting. Why you watch?'

The reason I watched them was the reason I did pretty much anything when I was thirteen: because all my peers did. These shows were what everyone in class talked about at school; I don't think I ever even considered whether I liked them any more than I'd ever considered whether I liked water: they were a vital part of my existence, a part of my survival. But at that moment, Fifi became the little boy pointing out the royal nudity, the Australian soaps were the naked emperor and I was the heretofore duped villager, and I saw them for what they were: ridiculous pantomimes with cardboard scenery that I spent five hours a week watching. As much as I'd like to say at this point that I promptly gave up watching the Australian soaps and never again bought a *Neighbours Annual* book, that would be a lie (come on – we're talking social ostracism in the fourth form here). But I was at least now a little discomfited by it and it did make me become more self-aware and questioning about why I did things. So *merci*, Fifi. It almost makes up for the weekend you made me spend at Eurodisney.

This, in a sense, is what I've tried to do with this book: be like my French exchange and point out that some things do not need to be. And as for the things that do unavoidably need to be, I'll suggest ways in which they can be rendered more bearable.

Now, before you dive off from the steps of this introduction and into the swimming pool of the book itself, I must warn you of something. There is a fair amount of sex talk in this book. Sorry, Mum and Dad/You're welcome, everyone else! This was not exactly my intention when I set out to write this book, and, in fact, I didn't even notice it until I reread the finished product and I'll admit I was, if not clutching a white lace handkerchief to my lipsticked mouth, a touch surprised. My general attitude to sex is similar to the one I have to exotic travel: happy to experience it as an activity, somewhat less interested in reading about it.

But then, it was inevitable (maybe). My conscious intention in writing this book was to address some of the clichés and tropes that can, all too easily, shape one's expectations of life and oneself, and Lord knows there are a lot of clichés about sex and how it should feature in a woman's life. So what I'm saying is this: I've written the words 'blow job' a number of times here, but it's purely for professional purposes. And just to clarify, I don't mean that in a prostitutional way.

Seeing as I started this introduction with an eighties film quote, I'd like to end with one. It took Bill S. Preston esquire, Ted Theodore Logan and Abraham Lincoln a journey through time in *Bill and Ted's Excellent Adventure* to learn the lesson that one should 'Be excellent to one another.' It's not a bad motto to live by, but I'd timorously like to suggest that there is something else that is arguably more important. I know a lot of women who are excellent to other people but feel less than excellent in themselves. Anyway, 'excellent' suggests, to me, perfection. Fuck that. Be strong, be confident, be good to yourself. Be awesome.

The office of magical thinking

Here are five of rules of thumb, should all the fingers on one of your hands turn into thumbs and you decide to rule them.

1. There is no day too dull, no problem too great that cannot be fixed with a couple of plays of 'Rush Rush' by Paula Abdul.
2. The amount of time it takes for you to get over him is exactly the same amount of time it will take for him to start missing you.
3. Talking about exercise burns exactly the same amount of calories as doing exercise.
4. 'When someone asks you if you're a god, you say YES!'
5. The office sucks.

Four of these are true. And one – is wrong! Damn wrong!

'Yay, I'm in the office!' is not a sentence one frequently hears, or at least not uncoated in the gloopy marinade of heavy sarcasm. 'Yeah, I'm stuck in the office,' is the more common phraseology.

Indeed, 'an office job' is often held up as precisely the opposite of human aspiration. 'Pen-pusher', 'office lackey', 'wage slave': the derogatory terms for a person devoted to the office life are many. The only positive one, really, is 'boss', and even that's only a good thing if it's you that has the title.

Oh sure, there is the whole 'trapped sitting at the same desk every day, year upon year, watching your life go by as you work in this soul-crushing, dehumanising place doing a wholly pointless job' element. Then there's what Joshua Ferris described in his office-based novel, *Then We Came to the End*: 'sitting all morning next to someone you deliberately cross the road to avoid at lunchtime'. (Although as true office devotees know, you don't go out to eat your lunch: you eat at your desk while surfing the internet, thereby reducing your daily movement to a level one can only describe as 'paraplegic'.)

But in the main, antipathy towards the office is merely a hangover from the teenage mentality that dominates so much of adult life. An example of this is the frisson that exists around alcohol twenty years after one is allowed to drink it legally, expressed in the faux-shamefaced boasting about how hilariously wasted one was the night before. You know, only really COOL people are allowed to buy alcohol.

But the most obvious manifestation of this mentality is in regard to the office. To work in an office is the adult equivalent of studying for an English test and giving the answers that you know will get you a decent grade as opposed to riffing off on your own torturously thought-out theories to express your individuality (working in the creative arts); crossing your fingers and hoping for the best (freelancing); or cheating (living off someone else). It's the coward's way, in other words, the approach that is boring and safe, in which the reliability of the outcome is in no way worth the monotony of the process.

But like telling the teacher what they want to hear in order to get on with your life as quickly and painlessly as possible, the office is deeply underrated. Far from being the place where your soul goes to die, it is the ideal environment for the human being, providing occupation, companionship, identity, shelter, food and water; in other words, all anyone needs to survive physically and emotionally. It is the Serengeti to your inner pinstriped tiger. And, of course, it also has that most basic of human requirements, too, the one God gifted to Moses on the Mount: free internet access.

In order to appreciate this, you have to leave the Office of Conditioned Responses and transfer yourself to the Office of Magical Thinking, and to help facilitate this, all your concerns will now be dealt with by HR, point by point. Tea and coffee will be available. Well, they are wherever you are reading this, presumably. And if they're not, then this book is insulted that you are reading it in such a poor environment. No wonder you have trouble in the office, you anti-social weirdo.

1. 'Office life is so predictable and always the same!'

Along with Manhattan and Paris, the office is one of only three places on earth that looks EXACTLY how it is portrayed in the movies. *The Apartment, Working Girl, Being John Malkovich, Wall Street, Office Space, Lost in America, The Secret of my Success*: all these movies are not just set in offices but are pretty much predicated on the fascinating dynamics thereof. Not always in a positive manner, admittedly, but still. Do you know how hard it is to break into the movies?

The filmmakers do not prettify or uglify the offices as they do to, say, London, but rather keep them looking wholly realistic and utterly recognisable, meaning, ergo and thusly, that the office is inherently perfect. Any of those offices could be your office, if your office had people in it who look like Harrison Ford and with the comic timing of Jack Lemmon.

But whereas the synchronicity between the cinematic and the reality is seen as proof of Manhattan and Paris's miraculous aesthetics, with skyscrapers that twinkle in the night like promises and elegant cobbled streets lit by Beaux Arts street lamps, it is seen in a somewhat less affirmative light in regard to the office, with its aisles of filing cabinets bedecked with three-month-old Styrofoam coffee cups with odd semicircle chunks ripped out along the rims.

Whenever a location scores a long-term gig to appear onscreen, this is generally considered an enormous compliment to the venue. So great, even, that it may become something of an annoyance to those who dwell there in real life, judging from the sign outside the house in New York that was used as the setting for Carrie's apartment in *Sex and the City*. Across the beautiful high steps that front this elegant brownstone house is a long thick chain and on which a sign hangs that snarls, pit bull-like: 'Tourists: FUCK OFF.' I paraphrase, but only slightly.

Yet even though the office setting has appeared in more films than desert islands, no one ever stands in the middle of an office, arms akimbo, digital camera at the ready and says, 'Wow, it's just like being in a movie!'

So the office slogs on. It is the location equivalent of one of those great character actors who everyone dimly recognises but no one appreciates, who gets steady work but never a good table at Spago's. Really, what does a location have to do to get some validation in this town?

This outrageous double standard is a tragedy, not just because it has blinded that ultimate peddler of visual clichés, Woody Allen, to the obvious idea of making an office-based movie;* it also means millions, nay, BILLIONS of people fail to realise, daily, that, far from throwing their lives down the plughole of monotony, they are living the Hollywood dream. Mia Farrow in Allen's *The Purple Rose of Cairo* had to wait for an invitation from Jeff Daniels before she could step into the world of cinema. You, on the other hand, get to do it effortlessly five days a week, every week, until the day you die. Isn't that awesome?*2

---

* An interchangeable leading actor, doing his best Woody Allen impression, is stammering and tugging his hair as he tries to work the photocopier; an inappropriately young actress sorts it out for him, but notwithstanding her technological wizardry, her personal life is a mess and she is prone to inexplicable displays of over-emotion; even though he fails to hold any obvious attractions – physically, emotionally, intellectually, personally – all the women in the office are just crazy for this self-obsessed stammerer, and he valiantly battles them away, except for the implausibly predatory teenage office intern who he is pretty much forced to sleep with; the women who are his age who want to sleep with him, on the other hand, are uniformly depicted as crazy, embarrassing and damaged (but not in a sexy way); at the office Christmas party the over-emotional woman turns up with her husband but after a conversation with the stammering man during which he repeatedly puts her down and mocks her ignorance of boring subjects like jazz and films about the Holocaust, she realises that he is the one for her; there is a showdown between the husband and the stammering man in the office, in which they run around the banks of desks and throw pencils at one another; everybody ends up exactly as they began and the stammerer continues to sleep with the teenage intern, raising the question what the point of this whole movie was anyway; the end.

*2 Rhetorical.

2. 'The office keeps me from pursuing my dreams!'

As anyone who works from home can tell you, unless your dreams are sitting at home, watching *Loose Women* and masturbating all day, the office is not keeping you from anything (and if you are ever tempted to do both of those activities at the same time, then it probably would be best if you stayed at home and out of society's way).

No doubt images of working to your own inner timetable instead of doing the 9–5 are dancing in your head: days that are peppered with spontaneous trips to museum exhibitions and mid-afternoon yoga classes in which you actually have space to do a warrior position, unlike in the overcrowded 6.30 p.m. classes in which all moves are accompanied by two slaps in the face and a kick in the butt from the people packed in next to you. Maybe you could even get on with writing that novel you've been thinking about for eight years but were prevented from starting by the office, yes, even on weekends, vacations and other days when you were not, literally speaking, in the office. It is still the office's fault that the world has not been gifted with your creative talents.

But such potential bonuses are the buttercream icing on your carrot cake, the occasional brilliant guest appearance on *Saturday Night Live*: insufficient compensation for a dreary base. Working from home requires relying on one's own self-discipline to work from somewhere that probably has many more distractions than an average office does as well as that cruel bitch of a siren, that battery-powered heroin: the TV remote.

If you should ever feel like maybe your home is getting a bit dull, then stay home to work one day and you will marvel at how you have been living in a veritable Disney World all these years without even noticing. Look at all these old copies of magazines you could spend the morning reading! And music playlists that need making! And old photos that require organising! (But don't stay home two days in a row because at that point your home will start to feel more like a prison and you'll probably have to move.)

Although the internet has now made shopping from the office possible, the threat of your boss walking up behind you generally acts as a dissuasion from clicking on net-a-porter and topshop.com more than twice an hour. The office is a similarly excellent preventative against obesity and food poisoning, if only because it is physically separating you from your fridge which, unlike the office canteen, is open for business allllll dayyyyyy lonnnnng. And, Jesus Christ, free! Free food – all day! How have you not noticed this before about your home? You would not believe how delicious that three-days-out-of-date pot of hummus will look when you have a deadline.

The downside to the free food, though, is that working from home will turn you feral. Never mind that old saw about not getting dressed until 2 p.m. if you work from home – try having to test your toothbrush for residues of wetness before opening the door for a delivery at 5 p.m. because you can't remember if you brushed your teeth today yet or not. That's when you know you have gone fully home-worker feral and you will probably never be fit to be socialised ever again.

In short, the office is daycare for adults. And do you know how much daycare for kids costs these days? And you're getting this daycare, not just for free, but for minus free in that they're paying you to be there! How totally baller is that?*

---

* Rhetorical.

15

3. 'I hate my job!'

I'm not here to help you love your job. I'm here to help you love the office. Next!

4. 'Everyone in my office drives me insane!'

You don't need to be a screenwriter for *The Office*, either the original UK or the far superior (whoa, controversial!) US version to know that there are little glimpses of joy to be found in the world of office dynamics. But you also don't need to have worked in an office for three decades to know that 'little glimpses of joy' means 'long stretches of intense irritation'.

Most humans like companionship but most humans would also like to choose who their companions are and not have to spend most of their waking hours with people they barely know and like less every day, for years and years and years on end. Arranged marriage is illegal in western countries yet at least in an arranged marriage you can get out of the house and away from your non-chosen one; there is no such escape in an office environment. In order to be able to do crazy things like eat and pay your rent, you need to spend long swathes of time with your assigned companions.* Irritation in these instances is inevitable, but not for the seemingly obvious reason.

The truth is, the natural human condition can be summed up as, 'increasingly irritated and resentfully unsatisfied'. This

---

* It is, in fact, a little like being a kept man or woman. If you want to make office life really exciting, pretend you're Vivian in *Pretty Woman* and someone is paying you to spend time with them all day, albeit without the sex, the 'big mistake' shopping excursions or the rich partner who looks exactly like Richard Gere, which is the only kind of man who picks up hookers in LA. That's a useful career tip, girls!

irritation comes from the gaseous formation, Irritationium, which resides behind everyone's eyeballs and when a human begins to roll their eyes, this is like turning a doorknob and opening the door to release the Irritationium. The first thing Irritationium does is seek out its opposite force, dopamine. When dopamine floods the brain, making you happy, Irritationium immediately follows it, dulling down your happiness receptors and sensitising the parts of your brain that make you aware of being bored, grumpy and in the line that is moving slowest. This is why, by the third day of being on the holiday of your dreams, the initial appreciation of the idyllic white sandy beaches and abject self-indulgence will have faded and all you'll be able to see is how that fat guy from room 202 always gets the best beach chair and that the waiter with the glasses never serves you first.

But Irritationium doesn't need dopamine to work. It is just as effective with black holes or, as you know them, wasted moments of boredom that you won't even remember at the end of the day, let alone at the end of your life. Nature abhors a vacuum and so Irritationium swiftly fills it with questions about why you ALWAYS get stuck behind the tall guy at the cinema.

Human beings need something on which to focus their irritation like they need toilets for their waste products: office colleagues are the receptacles for irritation that your entire being is constantly defecating. Thus, if one removes the colleagues from the equation, the irritation will not disappear; rather, it will merely require another receptacle and if one is working on one's own that receptacle will be you.

Why can't you ever focus for more than two seconds before flicking over to some stupid internet blog? God, where is that file – why are you always so freaking disorganised? You haven't changed since you were sixteen when you would lose your bike key every other day. Jesus, it's 11.15 – why in God's name are you eating lunch now?

These are just some of the delightful conversations you will have with yourself – your irritating, useless self – should you work alone and out of the office. The seemingly obvious solution is to become a TWITLO, or one of Those Who Insist on Taking their Laptop Out, inevitably to a chain coffee house, Apple Mac and Starbucks mug coordinated ever so zeitgeistly. But you will find that it takes on average 7.2 seconds for the Irritationium to arrive and you will become consumed with hatred for every single other person in the café, even more so than you ever were for your office colleagues. Thereon, you will spend at least four hours of every day wandering from café to café, on the impossible quest of a café that does not possess any patrons who annoy you, but enough patrons so you don't feel self-conscious working in the café. This is the Xanadu of the freelancer.

Just as working from home will begin to make you hate your increasingly prison-like home, so working on your own will make you hate yourself. Work in an office and your flat will be a soothing oasis, work with colleagues and you will be the only sensible one in a building full of crazies, morons and knuckle-crackers. As it is written in the Bible: 'The path to a happy life is strewn with obsessive hatred of others and a constant mental cloud of confusion about why your obviously superior skills and insight remain unappreciated.' All office workers know that. Right?*

---

* Rhetorical.

A day in your life in *Daily Mail* headlines

'Not so glam now! Hadley dares to leave the house at 9 a.m. without any make-up.' 'Hadley enjoys the sun in a denim miniskirt – but how old is TOO OLD to flaunt one's legs? Our top writers discuss.' 'Shadow or cellulite? Hadley flashes some unfortunate mottling as she gets on the bus.' 'Hadley wolfs down a croissant on the bus. Doesn't she know all that sugar and fat cause cancer?' 'Tea for two? No, just one, actually: sad Hadley cuts a lonely figure as she buys just one cup of tea in the office canteen.' 'Hadley flaunts her bombshell curves as she walks to her desk.' 'As Hadley's clothes struggle to contain her expanding figure we ask, why ARE rates of obesity for women rising?' 'Fashion faux pas! Hadley wears her favourite blue shoes for the THIRD day in a row. Doesn't she know she should be supporting young British designers?' 'Lady in red! As Hadley dons a new red top studies show that women are TWICE as likely to go into debt from compulsive shopping than men.' 'As Hadley spends another morning in the office, a top vicar writes: "Feminism has forced women to deny their natural maternal desires and pushed them into the workplace with disastrous consequences for our society."'

'Hadley and mysterious friend eat their sandwiches outside – but is there more to this friendship than meets the eye?' 'Maybe choose a salad next time! This unflattering photo shows that Hadley would do better cutting down on the carbohydrates for a while.' 'Lunch or baby bump? That is quite a tummy bulge – will there be a little Hadley soon?' 'Hadley and male colleague talk about "work" at Hadley's desk. Our resident body language expert analyses what their looks REALLY say.' 'Brain drain: Hadley has spent a total of seven hours in front of her laptop which, one doctor says, will "definitely" give her a brain tumour.'

'Eating the pain away: Hadley turns to her favourite chocolate bar to help her get through another lonely afternoon.' 'What a difference two decades make! The summer sun shows how much Hadley's skin has changed since this photo was taken twenty years ago.' 'Oh dear! Hadley changes into a pair of unflattering flat shoes for the commute home. Our style expert says a pair of four-inch nude heels would suit her heavy legs better.' 'Wash your hands! As Hadley gets the bus home, our tests prove that she will encounter over 10,000 germs on public transport, all of which can cause cancer.' 'House price horror: a top estate agent claims, "Single women like Hadley hogging flats that families need has had a crippling effect on the value of properties in neighbourhoods across Britain."' 'As Hadley tries to drink her cares away with friends after work we ask, why ARE women reaching for the bottle so much these days?' 'Worse for wear, Hadley stumbles home after ANOTHER night out. But, warns a former self-described feminist, these not-so-young women will regret their selfish, irresponsible behaviour.' 'As unlucky in love Hadley goes to bed alone again, a top scientist estimates how many fertile years she has left – and you'll be SHOCKED by the answer.' 'Lullabye baby? Hadley sleeps soundly which, one nurse says, is a common sign of the early stages of pregnancy.'

Sex tips for smart ladies

Woo, sex!

Living, as we do, in such a sexually open and unrepressed society, pretty much every fetish is catered for in at least one medium or, more likely, all media. Heavily pregnant women, men dressed as babies, heavily pregnant women suckling men dressed as babies – images of whatever turns you on can be found in your newsagent, on your TV and on your computer at any time of the day, and you can enjoy them all in triple vision and, yes, I did only just resist writing 'as a threesome'.

Now, some might query whether we really do live in such a sexually unrepressed society. After all, they might say, one need only glance at the local multiplex to disprove this claim: when a movie featuring sex is seen as potentially more damaging to children's minds than one that shows non-stop, consequence-free violence and is rated accordingly, then that country still needs to readjust its value system out of the Savonarola setting in which it appears to be stuck.

Moreover, these perverted devil's advocates could continue, when the ideal female body according to the celebrity world and the glossy magazine trade has about the same amount of body fat as an underfed child and the firm breasts of a Barbie doll, whose primary function is to have babies ('IS JENNIFER ANISTON PREGNANT????') but then to obliterate any physical sign on their body that they were ever pregnant as soon as they give birth ('Nicole Kidman back in her jeans just three weeks after giving birth!') in a manner not that dissimilar to societies that banish women to a special hut during menstruation (ew, women showing physical signs of being grown-up women that don't involve men having sex with them – gross), that country cannot really then sneer at other cultures for their screwy attitudes to women and sex.

And finally, the sexual deviants could conclude, the fact that sex is still such an object of obsession, used to advertise all manner of unsexy products from chewing gum to movies starring someone called Ryan Reynolds, when the cover of a recent *Vanity Fair* magazine* celebrating how brilliant TV is these days depicted four talented actresses lying apparently naked in bed (because that's how people watch brilliant TV, you know: mid-Sapphic orgy), this suggests that modern society isn't quite so unrepressed as it likes to think. Taking away the taboo of sex might have taken away the stigma but did not lessen the fascination. Ubiquity of sexual imagery and references is not quite the same as sexual sophistication. In fact, some could say it is the diametric opposite.

To these people I say, yeah, but have you seen the cover of *GQ* this week? Some chick from a TV show is wearing an unbuttoned men's shirt – like she just had sex! And now can't

---

* May 2012.

find her clothes! – and is pointing her finger at her mouth! I said, POINTING HER FINGER AT HER MOUTH! I wonder what else she'd like to put in her mouth, eh eh eh! Simone de Beauvoir WISHES she lived in such a sexually sophisticated time!

Yet, amazingly, despite all the talk about sex, images of sex and songs about sex that form the backdrop to most people's daily lives (it is literally impossible to get from your front door to your office in the mornings without bumping up against at least seventeen references to sex. FACT), some people are not having their sexual needs slaked. This is not a proper state of affairs. After all, if there's one thing we all learned from John Updike it's that an author can get a surprising number of critical accolades if he writes with his penis. And if there's one other thing we learned from Updike it's that everyone should feel free to express their sexual needs and fantasies (especially if those fantasies are about how your neighbour's wife clearly wants to bang you, even though you look more imp than human).

So it is time to attend to the needs of these poor, sexually uncatered-for people because at the moment they languish, their desires unsatisfied, their daily lives freighted down with the shaming awareness that their musings are not just uninteresting but downright unimaginable to even the most extreme of porn merchants. Pictures of women fucking furniture? Stories about men getting blow jobs from their dogs? Please – I can see such things from my front window. No, I'm talking about a far more specialist need. I'm talking about … sex tips for smart ladies.

Granted, just that phrase, 'sex tips for smart ladies', will not, in all probability, have you sighing with orgasmic pleasure. If anything, it will likely have you crossing your legs and covering your ears faster than if you heard your mother sighing with orgasmic pleasure.

But this phrase will not be used in its usual manner, that is, as a euphemism for 'getting unnecessarily gynaecological', 'making women sound like morons' or for a genre of literature that appears to exist solely to reassure men who use prostitutes that, really, they're doing those gagging-for-it ladies a favour (feminism, you can go home now: your work here is done).

Part of the problem here is that while references to sex get more ubiquitous by the day, intelligent discussions about sex often feel as difficult to find as they were in the sixteenth century. Anything that claims to talk about female sexuality in a modern, smart and honest way is guaranteed to be brain-bleedingly obvious and crude (women masturbate! They have discharge! Tampon and penis traffic jams! Ha ha!), depressingly reductive and clichéd (men! They're terrible at sex! Ha ha!) or will take an accepted truism and amp it up so that whatever nub of truth it once contained is now hidden beneath all the attention-seeking bells and whistles with which it has been decked. ('Women love sex! Therefore, some women really love being paid for sex!' as one recent trend in literature, which apparently existed solely to reassure men who use prostitutes that they're doing women a favour, had it. Feminism, you can go home now, your work here is done.)

The most skating glance at *Cosmopolitan* magazine shows not just how little progress there has been in the last few decades when it comes to talking about women and sex, but how any progress that has been made has been in reverse gear. Oh, how starry-eyed that magazine once was! When Helen Gurley Brown assumed editorship of *Cosmopolitan* in 1965, she aimed to verbalise female sexual liberation and, for a time, she did just that. Now this once zeitgeisty publication runs features that range – as articles for women about sex generally do – from the inane to the obvious, e.g., '50 Great Things to do with your Breasts' ('Cook Dinner Topless, Apply a Little Tomato Sauce to your Nipple – Make Sure it's not too Hot – and ask your Man if it's Spicy Enough') and 'How Do I Have Phone Sex?' (spoiler alert: you don't have sex with your phone). I did not make those examples up.*

This is the glossy magazine equivalent of the cinematic degeneration from Katharine Hepburn and Cary Grant repartee to 'romantic' 'comedies' today that infantilise and humiliate women and star some actress who is down to her last couple of mill and so takes the pay cheque to present the most degrading portrayal possible of her gender, one that serves only to validate the assumptions of her male-dominated industry. Yes, it's great that so many movies focus on women's stories, and it's great that magazines can talk about women's sexuality so openly; unfortunately, many do so in such a manner that one wonders if the progress was a Trojan horse for misogyny.

Yet while there is literally endless talk about sex and depictions of sex in popular culture, there is next to nothing that treats it in a manner that might be useful to a halfway sentient person, and by sentient I mean a person who not

---

* To be fair to *Cosmopolitan*, its, shall we say, limited concept of feminism does mirror that of the woman most associated with the magazine. While Brown commendably encouraged women to enjoy their self-sufficiency and sexuality, the emphasis on pleasing men was soon seen to undermine the point. By the nineties she was urging women who suffered from sexual harassment, including Anita Hill – who in a high-profile case accused Supreme Court Judge Clarence Thomas – to 'just shut up. Leave the poor guy alone. Did it kill them?'

only doesn't fancy dunking her nipples in a jar of spaghetti sauce but requires warning to test the temperature.

Thus, it feels especially difficult to ask what would now be deemed a relatively basic-level sexual enquiry. How can one ask, at the age of twenty-seven, how to give a hand job when surely by that age you've had sex swinging from chandeliers, right? (A note about chandelier sex, by the way: watch out for the candles.)

This has led to the ridiculous situation of there being sex experts in pretty much every mainstream newspaper and magazine but a near dearth of any useful or even realistic advice because just to publish a letter from a reader asking for hand job tips would make the newspaper look as anachronistic as if it were published on a stone tablet. Far better to publish one asking what to do when one fantasises about having sex with his mum.* That's so much more *au courant.*

Yet just because it feels like there are so few answers out there does not mean some women don't still have questions. Which brings me to the night I went to a sex class.

Not very long ago, I attended an evening class in the sex shop at the end of my road. It was, as Snoopy would say, a dark and stormy night (lawyer's note: Snoopy never went to a sex class). A dark and stormy Monday night, in fact. I'll call the sex shop the Cunning Linguist, because that is pretty much the level of ingenuity the owners applied when naming their shop. Apparently, poor punning skills are not generally seen as an ominous reflection of abilities in other areas because the class was packed with twenty- and thirty-

---

* 'I sometimes thought I was having sex with my mother when I was in bed with my girlfriend. Is that normal?', *Guardian*, 29 July 2011.

something women, all sitting amid the store's rails of dildos and strap-ons, notebooks primly on their laps, ready to take notes and draw diagrams. Despite or, yes, because of the ubiquity of sex talk in the world, a lot of women still feel incredibly insecure about certain aspects of sex, and when I say that the class's name was Blow Jobs to Blow the Mind!, you'll have an idea of what one of those things generally is.*

Unfortunately, by the end of the two-hour class few questions were answered because the teacher and former porn actress, Madam Kim ('You might have seen some of my work? No?'), was less interested in explaining the basics and a lot more interested in namedropping the extremely well-endowed porn stars she'd worked with ('Dean Danners! Dean fucking Danners! None of you have heard of him? None?'), spinning theories about natural design ('There's a reason God made your arms long enough to reach the crotch. Think about it') and describing in extraordinary detail a former colleague whose speciality was triple anal penetration, which seemed to me the complete opposite of what this class's exclamation-marked name promised.

In defence of Madam Kim, part of the problem might have been the subject. Perhaps there are only so many ways to skin a cat, so to speak. Bless her, she tried to zhoosh things up a bit, coining all sorts of terms such as 'the taco hold', 'the clam' and 'the envelope' that we all dutifully wrote down in our notebooks, but, even from my vantage point in the front row, they did all look exactly the same, even after I'd moved aside the giant pots of lube that had previously been partially

---

* I am sure many men feel insecure about sex, too. However, despite having been to a sex class, I can only deal with one gender at a time. I'm vanilla like that.

blocking my view. Madam Kim appeared to concede the point when she told us the best thing for us to do was to come up with our own tricks, which is surely like telling someone who has come over to stay the night to go to the bathroom and masturbate and leave you in peace.

At one point she paused, lost in wonderment at the memory of a former colleague's 'most beautiful asshole', and one of my classmates took advantage of the moment to ask a question: 'Um, when you're giving a blow job, how do you stop yourself from feeling like you're going to puke?'

Judging from the chorus of relieved murmurs around her, this was the question the majority of the class had given up their Monday night to have resolved.

Madam Kim looked like Frank Sinatra being asked to sing 'My Way' again, if Sinatra gave up crooning in his dotage and moved on to Italian opera.

'Uh-huh, sure. Well, you just gotta keep telling yourself he loves it. That's a real turn-on. HE LOVES IT. Thinking that really helps to open the throat,' she replied, slipping over the surprisingly slender line that divides self-empowerment and self-abasement when it comes to discussion about female sexuality. And then she went back to talking about the time she gave Dean Danners's twelve-inch cock a clam hold.

Of course, why anyone would trust the wisdom of someone who labours under the occupation name of 'sexpert' is a reasonable point. Yet seeing as depictions and discussions of sex in pop culture have so roundly failed to keep pace with sexual liberation, it would be useful if someone out there could offer sensible advice. Someone, ideally, who does not speak in the dreaded newspaper sexpert tone which generally makes me want to vomit without anything at all in my mouth: palpably hushed with self-conscious solemnity and po-faced faux maturity, rather like a teacher reading out a note in front of the class that is full of dirty words. 'This is a very serious subject,' the tone intimates. 'And anyone who laughs is simply revealing their own immaturity.' As an irritation factor, it is rivalled only by the Sexpert Minxy Byline Photo: 'Yes,' say those pursed lips, those lowered eyelids, 'I've had A LOT of sex. See how wild and loose my hair is? It's because I've just had sex. See how I'm holding this pen in my photo? Just imagine what else I could hold so masterfully. See how my shoulders are bare. That's because I just had sex. You hear me? Sex.'

Again, speaking purely from a personal perspective, they act like the image of Boris Yeltsin squatting naked on a coffee table used to act on Wayne and Garth from *Wayne's World*: the ultimate schwing-killer.

Whether pop culture's sniggering voyeurism and retrograde misogyny reflect most people's attitude to sex is a bigger question. They encourage that tendency, certainly, as anyone who has ever, despite themselves, bought a tabloid because of a front page story involving a footballer and his alleged 'mid-romp' puking (thank you, Ashley Cole) knows. But at the risk of upsetting every tabloid journalist who makes a living out of assuming that the thought of other people having sex is the most mind-bogglingly shocking concept this side of the Higgs boson particle, I'm going to say that, ultimately, no, it isn't, or no more than Pringles reflect the human need for regular nutrition.

Well, at last, all those sex questions you've always wondered about will be answered and you won't have to suffer a Sex Therapist Tone, Minxy Photo or tales of triple anal penetration to hear them. You're welcome!

✱ Hey, why doesn't the guy ever offer to put on a condom? Why is it always my job to tell him? I mean, it goes ON HIM, right? Even in the rare film that admits, yes, condoms are worn during sex, it's still the woman who has to prompt the man. It's not like I'm expected to tell a man to shave in the morning or to do any of his other manly self-care tasks, and I don't expect him to tell me to put in a tampon, or whatever. So why this craziness, why why why?

Easy: it's a little-known fact among the female populace, but a very well-known one among the male populace, that men cannot get sexually transmitted diseases. That's right: just as they cannot get pregnant, so they cannot get herpes, genital warts, hepatitis, gonorrhoea, syphilis, HIV (am I turning you on yet?) and so on. Men also cannot pass on any STDs because none of them – not one of them – has an STD.

Moreover, if a guy doesn't want to get the woman pregnant, he literally won't get her pregnant. Isn't that amazing? He just transmits a thought down to his penis mid-sexual encounter that says, 'Penis, listen to me: I want to get laid but I don't want a baby. So don't shoot out the good stuff.' And it won't! Ah, the wonders of science.

So seeing as sex is consequence-free for a guy, why would he sheathe the mini-me?

Oh wait, what's that? I'm getting word from a medical-type person that this isn't the case. They CAN get STDs too? And pass them on? And they can't telepathically send thoughts to their penises? Huh. So why –? Because they can't get pregnant? And therefore they don't grow up thinking of sex as having any consequence other than an orgasm? And because many of them think that, well, the woman can sort it

– there are pills, right? And she's probably on the Pill anyway, right? And because many of them live in the mistaken belief that it is very hard for men to catch STDs from women? Or pass them on? Because such things don't happen to guys like them? And because they just don't want to wear a condom? And because some of them, in the moment (and possibly beyond), are selfish jerks who are just thinking about one thing right then and it ain't their health, let alone her health? And maybe this should make the woman think twice whether this moron deserves the privilege of gazing upon her naked body seeing as he has so little interest in its physical wellbeing? Oh. OK.

Hope that clears it up for you.

★ **How long is it normal for a single woman to go without having sex?**

Gosh. Well. THAT'S embarrassing. How long are we talking here?

★ **Oh, um, I didn't realise I'd have to say. Well, there was this guy last summer but his, um, didn't really go in, um –**

STOP! I was just kidding! Please, I beg you, stop making those gestures with your fingers!

Contrary to common perception, one's attractiveness is not measured in how many people have seen you naked. It's actually measured in the quality of your dance routine to 'She's Like the Wind' by Patrick Swayze. Personally, I'm VERY attractive.

As to how long it's normal to go without having sex, the thing to remind oneself here is that the human body is not a car. It doesn't need regular top-ups of, um, a certain viscous liquid that comes out of a nozzle which is inserted – whoa horsey! Sorry about that, I got carried away with my own metaphor. Let's just say, your body is not reliant on regular top-ups, and we'll stop there. In fact, it can run on empty for years and years and years. I realise this goes against the wise words preached by Owen Wilson and Ben Stiller ('Seriously, do you, like, service yourself ten times a day?'), but this is one of those rare occasions, maybe even the only occasion, on which one must disregard the Holy Book of *Zoolander*.

Sex is, yes, a natural physical impulse, and while it might be necessary for most people to have mental equilibrium and feel a sense of fulfilment, it's not actually essential to maintain bodily functions.

And yet, just as the so-called sexual revolution may have opened the gates to talking about sex and yet not actually raised the levels of maturity and intelligence in how sex is discussed or viewed, so it took away the social stigma of sex happening beyond the bounds of wedlock but seemed to replace it with a stigma of sex not happening outside wedlock. In other words, retained the sexual obsession, just transferred it over to the other side. If *The Scarlet Letter* were written today, it would be about an attractive twenty-something woman who went for eighteen months and counting without getting laid. Stone her out of town, the repulsive deviant!

This is because while a man not having sex is endearingly, even relate-ably tragic, a woman not having sex is simply tragic, worryingly pitiable, probably physically and almost certainly psychologically deformed. From *Sex and the City* ('If you don't put something in there soon it will grow over,' one character is warned after it transpires she hasn't had sex since her divorce a handful of months ago) to pretty much every women's magazine on your newsstand, the assumption is now that a woman has the freedom to go home with any of the similarly single chaps she meets at whatever dreary house party she finds herself at on a Saturday night, surely she will take advantage of that freedom.

Yet the freaky truth is that while, yes, women can now have casual sex without being pilloried, and yes, this is a very good and right and equal state of affairs, some women don't want to. Some women don't want to sleep with people they don't know all that well, even if it is on offer to them. Just because there is cake available at the buffet doesn't mean everyone is going to have a piece of the cake. It's not that you don't like cake (who doesn't like cake?), it's that you're not hungry right now, or maybe you don't like that flavour of cake and you'd rather wait to get home and fix yourself the kind of cake you know you do – OK, I'll quit the metaphors now.

Thus, if you are a woman who doesn't really enjoy casual sex and you are also rather picky when it comes to relationships, preferring to be with no one rather than just anyone as you're holding out for if not the One then at least someone, and are also rather shy or maybe a little self-conscious, you may indeed find yourself going without sex for, well, quite a while. And you know what? That's just fine. It's only because there is still such an immature attitude about sex that anyone would even think of judging that. Why not worry about when was the last time you went down a waterslide? Or read the latest David Sedaris article? Oh that's right, because it doesn't involve getting – giggle – naked. Well, I guess it could, but only if you didn't mind waterslide friction rash. And really liked David Sedaris.

But I get that sex has more of a frisson than waterslides (if not more friction). But instead of focusing on when you last had sex, or how many people you've had sex with, how about thinking instead, respectively, about when was the last time you had sex that was more good than awkward and how many people you had sex with who wouldn't cause you to hide behind a rubbish skip if you saw them on the street. And then once you've calibrated those figures, go back to learning the dance moves to 'She's Like the Wind'.

✷ **OK, I've had a one-night stand with someone in my office. How do I convey to him the next day that I soooo don't care about what happened and yet am open to it happening again but, you know, sooooo don't care about it? Really, I've actually already forgotten about it!**

You should walk past his desk as often as possible wearing as little as you can get away with while talking loudly into your mobile about all the guys who've asked you out recently (note: make sure you turn off your mobile when you do this. It is very embarrassing if one's phone rings while having a fake conversation).

Then wait for an occasion that will involve you and him and alcohol in the same room at the same time. In Britain, sexual advances can only be made under the forgiving umbrella of alcohol. That way, if rejection occurs on either side, before or after the encounter, you can both put the whole thing down to drunkenness. Christ, you didn't think I really MEANT to sleep with you, did you? Ha ha! This is known as faux ironic seduction and it is the only form of seduction the British can understand or accept. But even under the alcohol umbrella, you absolutely must not make any overt sign or, God forbid, declaration that you like this person. Drunken passivity is the name of the game here.

So in short, the answer is to act like a combination of Cher in *Clueless* when she's trying to attract a young man ('Sometimes you have to show a little skin. This reminds boys of being naked, and then they think of sex!'), Chandler from *Friends* and Hugh Grant in any movie: overly flirtatious, self-defensively ironic, unironically useless. And if that tack doesn't work, instead of questioning the methodology of not showing someone you like them in order to get them to like you, just say to your friends that 'it wasn't meant to be' and have them repeat it back to you until you almost believe it. Better that than actually being honest with someone and risking humiliation, right? You can't fight fate!

★ Now I've had another one-night stand with someone in the office and I really don't care about it. How best to proceed with maturity, dignity and professionalism?

Never talk to them again. The end.

★ How come in sex scenes in movies the woman almost never takes off her bra? Have I been doing it wrong all this time?

And why doesn't she ever have her period? That's what I've always wondered. Or maybe that's why Hollywood likes its actresses to be so thin: so the women never menstruate and can provide sex on tap.

Sex scenes are, of course, an essential part of pretty much every film, whether it's one about such unerotic subjects as the sinking of a giant ship (*Titanic*) or Tom Cruise and Nicole Kidman in a relationship (*Eyes Wide Shut*). Yet once the man and this never menstruating woman do have sex, the actress – unless she's Jamie Lee Curtis, circa 1984 – will refuse to take off her bra. So let's get this straight: the actors need to have sex because that, apparently, turns audiences on, so obviously the female character can't have her period or anything else that would impede the action. But actual breasts won't be shown unless the actress gets paid an extra $10 million. Meaning that, at most, audiences will be watching people who in real life probably hate one another and are maybe married to other people dry hump one another in their underwear. I don't know about you, but just talking about it is turning me on.

✱ **Speaking of the cinema, what are you supposed to do if you go to the cinema on a first date and suddenly there's a very graphic sex scene?**

Don't go to the cinema on your first date. Seriously, why on earth would you opt for an activity that involves the two of you sitting awkwardly next to one another in a darkened room, each afraid to laugh at the funny bits because you're worried whether the other person will judge you, plus with added sex scene risk? And it's not like you can pretend you need the loo during the sex scene because your date will either think you're a massive prude or that you've just snuck off to, to paraphrase *Zoolander* again, service yourself. Neither of these are things anyone wants their date to think, mid-date or ever. So if you find yourself in this situation, watching a sex scene on a first date, you may as well just run out of the cinema screaming, spraying popcorn all around you.

★ **So is it possible to give a blow job without feeling like I'm going to vom?**

Look, sometimes you'll feel like you're going to vom. Sometimes you'll feel spectacularly bored. Sometimes you'll hate it and wish you were doing literally anything else. And just occasionally, you will actually like it. Hey, it ain't called a job for nothing.

★ **Blow jobs are easy because a guy is grateful for any oral action you give him down there. But what about hand jobs – how do you do those?**

Why are you asking me? Ask the guy himself. He's had literally decades of experience tugging at the thing. I'm sure he'd be happy to demonstrate.

★ **Why are blow jobs a given but cunnilingus is a special treat?**

Because it's harder to spell. And because you are sleeping with selfish jerks. Next!

★ **Why is sex, of all physical desires and behaviours, the one freighted with so much guilt and fascination in that order?**

Yes, it is funny, that. Outside my window I can see Richard Dawkins, bless him, waggling his fists and bellowing, 'It's because of religion! It's because religion freighted down sex with so much guilt and fear out of men's paranoia about the paternity of their children and out of a way to control the populace! And they did this so effectively that even today, even people who haven't been in a religious building since their parents made them go through the traditional infant rites to placate the grandparents feel it too! Arg! Must! Get! Angry! On! TV! Again! Soon!'

But just before I slam down that window I lean out and shout, 'Oi! Dawkins! You've only got it half right! You've forgotten the American Pie factor! And a man of your intelligence, too. Sheesh!'

The American Pie factor – named in honour of the film, mind, and not the song – is the deeply embedded belief that sex proves one is a grown-up, one is desirable and one is cool. Of course, in that film the characters were eighteen whereas the large majority of the populace is not. In fact, the vast majority is older than eighteen. Nonetheless, their attitude to sex is not much more mature than that of the young chaps in that film.

So when you find yourself stuck in the dentist's waiting room and gazing upon the cover of another men's magazine in which an actress promotes her latest lame movie in that time-immemorial manner – posing in a pair of bikini bottoms while twisting up her T-shirt and talking about how much she loves freaky sex and how empowered she feels – ponder upon a parallel universe in which a different physical action other than sex was fetishised. Like, oh, let's say, defecation.

Movies would be censored for having too many bathroom scenes (with extra parental guidance urged for actual shots of the toilet); underground orgy parties would feature laxatives and excellent plumbing, and God only knows what the fetish gear would look like. Presumably chaps would still work. And pity the Catholic priests! The terrible bowel troubles they would suffer due to their mistaken belief that God has forbidden them to defecate. Some of them, somehow, would learn to twist their internal organs into such a way so as to adhere to this inhuman commandment, but many, many others would secretly try to find outlets to relieve their urges, outlets that would offend God far more than simply using the toilet.

The point of this little segue is not to promote coprophilia, but to point out how weird and, frankly, retrograde an obsession with sex is. To paraphrase the oracle on the subject, George Michael, yes it's natural, yes it's good, not everybody does it but everybody should. But, honestly, world, get over it. It's an obsession that ultimately causes pain to millions and millions and millions of others. It feeds into religions' cruel and weird fetishisation of it which then can damage its followers. It encourages the condescension of grown adults by pop culture. And finally, it leads inexorably, unavoidably to the Sex Therapist's Tone. So for all our sakes, grow up.

✷ **So I'm about to sleep with a new gentleman caller for the first time. Should I go get a Brazilian wax?**

Well, I don't really know. Is your gentleman caller a paedophile? A porn merchant? If so, then the state of your pubic hair is really the least of your problems. If not, no. So in short, the answer, in all scenarios, is no.

Before we get into the nitty-gritty of ladies' pubic hair, without, hopefully, finding anything nitty or, indeed, gritty in there, let us first get a grasp on the linguistics of the subject while struggling, ever so diligently, not to make any 'cunning linguist' jokes. I leave that to my local sex shop.

The bikini wax is, as its Ronseal-does-exactly-what-it-says-on-the-tin name suggests, a wax around the sides so that one can go to the beach without sparking too many comparisons to Grendel's mother.

The Brazilian is a very extreme bikini wax, leaving one with just a mere centre line of pubic hair which some people insist on referring to as 'the landing strip' which in turn suggests that they only do missionary position.

And then finally, there's the full Brazilian, where absolutely everything is removed. This is also occasionally known as 'the Hollywood', which tells you everything you need to know about that town: it insistently remakes foreign products with American dialogue and it prefers its women to resemble Barbie.

Now, I am very much of the belief that, as long as it's legal, a woman should be allowed to do pretty much anything if it makes her feel happy and confident in herself and, yes, that does include the styling of her pubic hair. What she should not do, however, is feel pressurised to torture her genitals because she assumes that is what sexual partners and society itself expects of her. Yet at some unspecified point over the past twenty years, pubic hairlessness became a shorthand for mainstream female sexiness. Once women with hairless vaginas were something one saw on cards in public phone boxes. Now such a thought is as outmoded as the phone boxes themselves. If anything had to cross over from the porn industry, I wish it had been the commendably straightforward movie plots ('I'm here to fix your photocopier.' 'Great!') but, sadly, it turned out to be pouring hot wax around one's labia and ripping out the hair. Oh well.

Look, I am as susceptible to the daftest fashions as the next person who has a subscription to multiple fashion magazines and I accept that fashions and expectations change, even in the pubic hair industry, as such a thing does indeed seem to exist.

But the advocation of the Brazilian wax and in particular the Hollywood is where I throw down my copy of *Sunday Times Style*, sell my flat and move to a mud hut in the Hebrides and spend my days carving recorders out of twigs and playing 'Annie's Song' to passers-by. There is nothing fashionable about following a trend that is derived so wholesale from the porn industry, nor is there anything trendy in encouraging gentlemen callers to think of it as both sexy and a given.

I never thought about Brazilian waxes much when I lived in London in my twenties. In fact, I thought the only people who had them were crazy-eyed trophy wives who were forced to submit their bodies to all manner of indignities so as to stop their piggy-eyed husband from shagging the sloaney nanny too often. This is because I believed – and still believe – that the only kind of people who dislike signs of female sexual maturity are ridiculous, repulsive people. Here's a slogan to embroider on a pillow on a rainy Sunday: sexual maturity is an attractive quality in an adult.

When I moved to Manhattan in my thirties, though, I could barely move without some white-coated woman trying to rip out all my pubic hair.

Every time I went for a bikini wax I had to have lengthy discussions explaining that, no, I did not want hot wax poured inside me, nor did I want to return home afterwards with my knickers full of blood as though I'd just had a backstreet abortion. The beauticians looked at me as though I were a wholesome German hippy, explaining why I brush my teeth with a leaf and plait my underarm hair.

I did think for a much longer time than I ever expected to muse upon the state of my pubic hair whether it is hypocritical for me to be disgusted by the rise of Brazilian waxes (THE RISE OF THE BRAZILIAN WAXES: now there's a horror movie I'd like to see, if only for the poster) and yet get a bikini wax before any occasion that necessitated me wearing a swimsuit in public, and I decided that maybe it is, a little, but not truly. My objection to the Brazilian is that it is such a weird combination of the aesthetics of porn and paedophilia and it encapsulates so many of the very wrong ideas that exist about women, sexuality and sexiness. Bikini waxes, for me at least, have nothing to do with sex. They are about not wanting to flash my pubes on the beach, because while there are some things I don't mind sharing with the public (my pubic hair care, apparently), my actual pubic hair is not one of them. A bikini wax is about, at the very least, privacy. Tidiness, too, like brushing my hair (on my head, that is.) And for the record, I'm not all that keen on seeing men's pubic hair creeping out of those tiny Speedos on the beach. I am an equal opportunities prude.

Brazilians are a whole different pubic hair ballgame.

'You really should try it,' said the New York beautician, frustrated again in her pursuit to pour hot wax around my labia, 'your boyfriend will love it.'

'If he did, he would not be my boyfriend much longer,' I huffed, a retort that perhaps would have carried a bit more heft if I wasn't at that point lying prone on a table wearing paper knickers.

Why any woman would sleep with a man who likes their women to resemble porn stars or pre-pubescents is just one of the great mysteries of the modern bedroom, along with why is it called a one-night stand as surely some people must still do it lying down.

It is so obvious that impossibly high heels are nothing but a modern-day version of foot binding and the normalisation of Brazilian and Hollywood waxes is the twenty-first-century western version of genital mutilation that it feels incredible that this even needs to be said. No, Brazilian waxes do not involve a clitoridectomy and destroy any chance of a woman experiencing sexual pleasure (although awareness that one is sleeping with a man who likes his ladies to have childlike genitals might kill the buzz a little). But they do involve pouring hot wax all over a woman's vagina and ripping out her hair in order to turn on a man who has presumably spent at least 89 per cent of his life wanking over porn.

When I ask my New York female friends – smart, funny, seemingly normal women – who do this to themselves on a monthly basis why on earth they bother, they always give the same two answers:

1. 'It's because then he goes down on me more often. I mean, there is a lot of hair down there so it's only fair.'
2. 'Because it gives me sexual confidence.'

Both of these are, clearly, nonsense. In regard to the first answer, any guy who says he is not giving a woman oral sex because she has pubic hair is a lazy selfish jerk who is making a phoney excuse for being all take and no give, or is a paedophile. Take your pick, ladies! Yes, hair is closer to the main dish on a woman than it is on a man but I can think of other things a woman has to contend with when giving oral sex that a man does not. So next time a guy says he'll only go down on you if you get rid of all that hair say, 'Sure! But only if you shove a massive dildo down your throat every time I go down on you, right? THANKS.'

As to the second point, if you need to rip out your own vaginal hair to feel confident, your vaginal hair is not the problem.

Pubic hair is proof of sexual maturity and if your partner finds that a turn-off, you should probably reconsider that partner.

So, in short, no, you do not have to have a Brazilian to get laid. In fact, any guy who likes a Brazilian shouldn't be in your bed at all. So following that logic, having a Brazilian will actively prevent you from getting laid.

Don't be mean to your genitals. After all, they are so nice to you.

Movies lie – damn it, woman, they lie!

It took me a long time and a lot of inappropriately overdramatic dialogue before I realised that real life is not how it is depicted in the movies, and, to be fair to movies, they never claimed otherwise. To be fair to me, they just insinuated it.

In retrospect, I should perhaps have realised that, already by the age of twelve, I took movies too seriously when I woke up the morning after being voted prom queen of my summer camp (George W. Bush is not the only American to have attained power through possibly dodgy vote counting) and felt … disappointed. It didn't make any sense: how could I – not a popular girl ever, and certainly not at summer camp where popularity could only be bought by the double and, to me, foreign currencies of athletic prowess and sluttiness – be anything other than ecstatic after, against all odds, beating the far sportier and sluttier Tiffany Feiglestein? Even better, winning meant that I got to dance to a cassette of the *Dirty Dancing* soundtrack in front of the WHOLE CAMP (attention – ha!) with dreamy fourteen-year-old (older man!) Alex Zimmerman (call me!). But that was precisely the problem: that moment – me looking into Alex's eyes as the speakers blared that we were having the time of our lives, him looking over my shoulder for Tiffany Feiglestein with whom he would spend the rest of the night making out under the gym steps while I chatted with my arts and crafts counsellor about my planned future career in papier-mâché – was the perfect climax, the point when the end credits should have rolled and a power ballad should have struck up, sung by Jennifer Warnes, Peter Cetera and Christopher Cross, three singers whose presence on a soundtrack guarantees a quality film.

It's not that I consciously wished for death after the prom (I am more Molly Ringwald than Sissy Spacek); rather, on some level, I just didn't realise that the slog of life still continued after the triumph, especially after an achievement that is so frequently touted as the end goal in movies. Personally, I'm surprised more divorces don't happen the day after the wedding. Wait, you mean there's still more to this story? And it involves me having to go to the supermarket and pay taxes and wait for the bus? But I thought everything was supposed to be sorted and perfect now! Mother FUCK!

There is a soul-crushing number of differences between reality and the cinematic version thereof. I'm not even talking about the sad lack of musical montages in one's life; nor the rarity of someone (a kooky new friend, a romantic interest, a mystical old person, a wise child who will tell you where you have been going wrong all along) turning up in your life at the exact moment when you need them; nor the fact that you are probably separated by many more than six degrees from Kevin Bacon. But rather, the certain tropes movies lazily rely on that have, through overuse, become such clichés that they are part of popular culture and become a given so that they become the prism through which you see your life and, in doing so, ruin it. Let's un-ruin your life!

1. All men are constantly desperate for sex and women are the reluctant objects of their energetic pursuits

As is the case with pretty much any gender stereotype, this one is spectacularly unfair on both sexes. There are so many movies – and books, and TV shows and magazine articles – that operate under this premise that to list them all would render this book a size that would give the whole of the nineteenth century's literary world put together an inferiority complex. It is always the men and boys in movies who are desperate to lose their virginity (*American Pie*, *Meatballs*, *The Virginity Hit*) because for women, of course, not only is virginity not an embarrassment but a commodity, and women, such movies infer, aren't actually that keen on sex anyway and only do it to please the men. I like to think that Stephen Fry's infamous claim that 'The only reason women will have sex with [men] is that sex is the price they are willing to pay for a relationship with a man,'* came from watching *American Pie* too many times, doubtless in between his heavy schedule these days of tweeting and writing puff pieces about Apple products. And that, ladies and gentlemen, is how this generation's Oscar Wilde spends his time.

Leaving Stephen Fry to the side, this trope about men's desire for sex and women's reluctance to have it has nothing to do with reflecting whatever differences may or may not exist between men and women's sex drives (and some of us would argue that differences between sex drives are more

---

* *Attitude* magazine, November 2010.

individually based than gender based, but particulars are so much more finicky than sweeping generalisations). It might well have more to do with the fact that most filmmakers are men who need to justify their lack of sexual success by portraying women as terrifyingly frigid as opposed to, just maybe, resistant to getting naked with a self-obsessed filmmaker.

What it mainly has to do with is laziness when it comes to thinking up new narratives. This trope is a barely updated version on the premise of centuries-old fairy tales: a princess lies imprisoned in a tower, helplessly, virginally, and the prince vigorously pursues her, thwacking away through her thicket of celibacy (they didn't have bikini waxes in Once-Upon-a-Time). This in itself comes from the ancient and reassuring (to some men) idea that men are the pursuers and women are the pursued because women do not enjoy sex. That is the male preserve. Therefore, women won't ever be sexually unfaithful and the man can rest assured that, yes, all his wife's children must be his. Pizzas for everyone!

Now, clearly, *American Pie* et al. were not attempting to make some comment on paternity insecurities, but it is a shame that they unthinkingly made do with a cliché that comes from a misogynistic fear and is worn down to a nub through overuse.

Presumably, for men, one consolation for being portrayed as hopeless, hapless, desperate hound dogs is that it explains away all female rejection as merely the downside to them being delicate princesses (making any eventual scoring with them even more of an achievement). Nonetheless, it is pretty insulting to them.

For women, this trope, while seemingly, sort of, complimentary, can only be hurtful. First, there is the insinuation that a guy will sleep with anyone so, you know, your prince may have come but, to be honest, he would come with anyone. Then there's the very overt suggestion that frigidity is, ironically, sexually attractive and, of course, feminine. But most of all, if you are a woman, it makes sexual rejection even more humiliating than it already is.

I mean, Christ, how ugly must you be if he turned you down? A guy would probably have sex with a bagel. And the hole in a bagel is just nothing. Your vagina is less than nothing. You are disgusting.

Well, here's an amazing little secret: almost all women have been sexually rejected at some point, and the only ones who haven't are nuns although, thinking about it, seeing as they're the brides of Christ in what is, presumably, an unconsummated union, then they must have been rejected too. So there it is: at some point in every woman's life, a guy – possibly even Jesus – declined the invitation to the party in her pudenda.

It even – yes, even! – happens to women in relationships. Movies often depict women in relationships as being especially resistant to putting out to their poor desperate husbands or boyfriends. After all, the only reason women enter relationships is to steal men's sperm and make sure they don't die alone. So once you locked the guy down, phew, you don't have to bother with THAT any more! This in turn explains why the only roles open to women in comedies are the shrewish wife/fiancée who spoils all the fun or the hot single girl (who presumably will release her inner shrew once she gets that ring on her finger – *The Hangover*, *Knocked Up*). Any woman in movies who does have a high sex drive is usually depicted as laughable, desperate and possibly crazy.

However, back on Planet Real World, some women's sex drives are higher than some men's, and sometimes he simply isn't in what Sebastian the crab from *The Little Mermaid* would call 'da mood'. But because this is a scenario that so rarely gets portrayed in popular culture, it can feel unique, and uniquely shameful.

While being rejected probably won't rank as the experience you would choose to go back and relive should God grant the opportunity in the moments before death, it is actually, beneath the waves of mortification and disappointment, quite reassuring. Namely, it proves that men, actually, won't have sex with just anything. Thus, while this man at this moment might not choose to have sex with you, the next one who does, or the next time he does, is doing so because you're you, not because you happen to have a couple of hole-shaped openings on your body. Isn't that romantic?

2. Popular kids are evil and will end up miserable

One of the myriad reasons that *Ferris Bueller's Day Off* is such a remarkable movie is that it turns over so many cinematic stereotypes about teenagers, which is not, to be brutally frank, something one can say of many of the late and undoubtedly great John Hughes's movies.* For example,

---

* For purposes of professional respect, I am just going to ignore Mr Hughes's descent down the age range and ensuing descent in quality with his 1990s and early twenty-first-century films about children (*Curly Sue*, *Home Alone*) and infants (*Baby's Day Out*), and eventual slump into the animal kingdom (*Beethoven*). It is a personal and professional tragedy that Mr Hughes didn't just stop making movies in 1989 at *Uncle Buck* – known among Hughesologists as the beginning of the Kiddysoeic period – and enjoy the last twenty years of his life, living on his much deserved profits from his work in the 1980s thereon.

when Ferris, Sloane and Cameron* manage to evade grown-up supervision, they don't cause chemical havoc (*Weird Science*); they don't get high, dance on their desks to eighties music and sneak around school for no apparent reason (*The Breakfast Club*): they go to a French restaurant, a museum and a parade. These are not cunning teenagers enjoying a rare day of freedom, this is an elderly couple on vacation enjoying their final years of mobility.

This in turn reflects the most interesting stereotype that this film craftily overturns: that popular kids are inherently evil. *Ferris Bueller's Day Off* is the only movie – and certainly the only 1980s or 1990s comedy – I can think of in which a teenager who is deemed by his peers to be cool is not portrayed as a rich bullying jerk who will eventually get his or her comeuppance by being killed in a fight (*Edward Scissorhands*), losing a sports match (*Teen Wolf*), spending the rest of his life washing his former victim's car (*Back to the Future*), being humiliated at the school reunion (*Romy and Michele's High School Reunion*), being humiliated by and then having to go out with Judd Nelson (*The Breakfast Club*), being killed (*Heathers*), getting tricked into becoming fat (*Mean Girls*), sinking into probable alcoholism (*Pretty in Pink*), being humiliated at his own party (*Some Kind of Wonderful*), or working for ever for his dad (*Peggy Sue Got Married*). Underdogs are an obvious protagonist staple for most narratives because, obviously, the kid who is being bullied is more sympathetic than the kid who is doing the

---

* And perhaps the ridiculousness of the characters' names encouraged Hughes to think a little more outside his usual box for their behaviour, and I say that as someone whose name sounds not entirely unlike a first draft for Ferris Bueller.

bullying. But considering what a bad rep popular kids now have thanks to the movies, one could argue that they are actually now the underdogs.

Ferris Bueller is a slightly odd, funny, tech-smart boy with a weak spot for Wayne Newton. In short, he is exactly the kind of boy who is usually portrayed in films, and especially films by Hughes in the eighties, as the bullied geek. Duckie in *Pretty in Pink*, which came out right before *Ferris Bueller*, is basically the nerd version of Ferris, down to his sweater vests and fondness for singing along to old songs, and the fact that both characters are played by actors (Jon Cryer and Matthew Broderick) who look, quite frankly, identical only underlines this. Yet in *Ferris Bueller* – which Hughes directed, unlike *Pretty in Pink*, which he 'only' wrote – the geek inherits the earth.

That this film instead makes Ferris the hero of not just the school but the whole town is partly why it has proven to be so much more timeless than any of Hughes's other eighties teen movies: it is simply more original. Moreover, it is a much more satisfying fantasy for all the loner geeks who, one suspects, made and continue to make up a significant portion of Hughes's audience.

The cinematic stereotypes about high school kids and what happens to them after graduation are more well trodden than the taped-up glasses of the class dork beneath the foot of the school bully: popular kids are shallow tyrants whose social success will peak in their school years; dorks are sweet and smart and they will achieve eventual vindication. And, like the previous example about women being universally resistant to men's charms, this lazy convention almost undoubtedly has some of its roots in the autobiographies of male screenwriters who were, by and large, high school dorks. If Hollywood had an epitaph it would be The Revenge of the Nerds.

Some cool kids may indeed peak in high school and spend the rest of their lives 'thinking about Glory Days', as Bruce Springsteen once put it, a tad gloatingly, and as epitomised by the character of Billy, played by Rob Lowe, in *St Elmo's Fire*, doomed after college to a lifetime of wearing a bandana and making nonsensical speeches about the cosmos to Demi Moore (no wonder he gets depressed). But like all generalisations, this one is ridiculous.

As I've already said, I was by no means a popular kid (only in movies do kids with names like Hadley or Ferris attain mass popularity as teens), so this defence of popular kids is not some poorly disguised self-justification. But rather, it's just to point out that this trope, aimed at geeky, unconfident, oversensitive teenagers like the one I once was, is false consolation and that is worse than no consolation because it is a lie.

While some kids (and grown-ups, sadly) attain social success through bullying, luck of genetics, generosity with sexual favours and simple sporting prowess, most do it through two factors that are simultaneously far more complicated and far more simple: self-confidence and random chance. As to the first of these, yes, self-confidence in school is probably much easier to come by if you are excellent at sports; it is harder to attain if your only talents are – oh, let's say, just off the top of my head – not needing to wear a bra until you're eighteen and knowing all the words to the theme song of *The Fresh Prince of Bel Air*. But it's the confidence that brings the coolness, not the athletic ability.

Curtis Sittenfeld's brilliant first novel, *Prep*, is the literary equivalent of *Ferris Bueller* in regard to this subject and also, come to think of it, in giving the characters some truly extraordinary names. So although some of the cool kids in her book are awful, the main ones – the unforgettably monikered Cross Sugarman and Gates Medowski – are simply blessed with preternatural self-confidence. All that holds back *Prep*'s protagonist, Lee, is her painfully heightened self-consciousness, and the fact that this novel became a bestseller suggests widespread recognition of the nugget of truth in the novel's narrative.

Yet for every *Prep*, there are about a million *Mean Girls* and these movies, however well intended, reinforce the rigidity of the school caste system because they teach geeky kids that there is no chance of them ever crossing that social barrier, certainly not without the very high risk of mockery and possible physical assault. The best they can hope for is eventual professional success, which smacks oddly of fanatical religious doctrine: suffer now, reap the benefits later. Becoming president of a computer company, enjoying seventy-two virgins in heaven – you say tomayto, I say tomahto.

These movies also suggest that being an outcast at school endows one with moral superiority as an adult, which explains the cliché of successful actresses and models (Cameron Diaz, Jennifer Aniston …), claiming in interviews that they were geeks in high school, a claim that is usually followed by an insistence that, honestly, they just can't resist French fries.

Prep, like *Napoleon Dynamite* – the other side to the *Ferris Bueller* coin – was brave enough to point out that, actually, not all dorks are adorable martyrs with encyclopedic knowledge about indie music and inherent academic genius. They are humans. This means some are nice and some are not and some are president of the physics club and some don't know how to spell physics.

But again, these are the exceptions. The more common approach is to insinuate that the school outcasts are the ones who will grow up better, richer and happier.*

In other words, these movies are saying that, actually, it DOES matter what group you were in at school, and it apparently matters even more than the bitchiest queen bee even realised in her heyday because its importance lasts beyond graduation day.

To buy into the idea that it matters a jot what social set anyone belonged to in school, and that it has any bearing on what that person was like at school and is like now completely nullifies any success you get in later life that you can flash at your next school reunion: you've already let the bullies win.

3. You have to be the boring woman to get the guy

Of all the film tropes, this is the one that consistently makes me the saddest. Not because I believe it (any more), but because it has ruined my enjoyment of so many otherwise great movies. I call this trope Tootsie's Law.

Now, *Tootsie* is a movie that is, in a lot of ways, amazing. This 1982 film cheerfully and fearlessly overturned a lot of received Hollywood wisdom such as, most obviously, that audiences would be repulsed by a movie featuring a man dressed as a woman. Even *Some Like It Hot* went black and white because director Billy Wilder feared that Tony Curtis and Jack Lemmon's make-up was just *de trop*, and this from a

---

* See *Peggy Sue Got Married*, *Romy and Michele's High School Reunion*, etc., etc.

movie that ends with Lemmon sailing off into the sunset with a man – IN 1959.

Far from worrying whether mainstream audiences could cope with the combination of foundation and stubble, *Tootsie* opens with close-ups of Dustin Hoffman putting on make-up and gleefully carries on from there, peaking perhaps with Hoffman standing in his girdle in one scene and debating with Bill Murray whether a certain dress makes him look 'hippy'. I love this movie.

One thing I don't love about it, though, is Hoffman's character Michael's love life. For those who haven't seen this film, first, I envy the pleasure awaiting you as you lose your *Tootsie* virginity. Second, I shall explain.

Relatively early in the movie, Michael sleeps with his long-term friend, Sandy, played by lovely Terri Garr, who is thirty-four, a struggling actress and hilarious, and afterwards he treats her – as he treats all women he sleeps with – like crap.

Meanwhile, Michael has recently got a job on a soap opera by pretending he is an actress as opposed to an actor and there meets one of the stars of the show, Julie, played by Jessica Lange. Julie is in a relationship with the lecherous director (played, of course, by Dabney Coleman), has an annoying breathy voice, a changeable southern accent and, damningly, is not funny, interesting or smart – in fact, she herself says she is dumb, and she's right about that (every woman knows you should never get involved with a character played by Dabney Coleman). She is also not the least bit interested in Michael, mainly because she thinks he's a woman. Needless to say, Michael falls in love with her, treats Sandy even worse and the movie ends (spoiler alert: but you might have already guessed this) with the rather implausible suggestion that gold-digging, breathy-voiced

Julie will now have a relationship with the broke and chronically out-of-work Michael who, for the past few months, has been dressing like Mrs Doubtfire.

I appreciate that questioning the credibility of the ending of a film that is based on the premise of no one in America noticing that a high-profile TV actress is Dustin Hoffman in a dress might seem like protesting that *Wizard of Oz* is not realistic because monkeys can't fly. But the point is not the realism but the overall trope, the one that says the boring pretty woman gets the man and reforms his womanising ways and the one who has an actual personality gets not just nothing but sidelined out of the entire film.

Another woeful example of this film-ruining trope is *Ghostbusters 2*, a movie that probably most people have forgotten about but, like a female Martin Scorsese I shall now restore to public consciousness.

One of my favourite dynamics in the original *Ghostbusters* film is the relationship between awkward egghead Egon, played by Harold Ramis, and the amazing secretary, Janine, played by Annie Potts. The final scene when she runs up to embrace him after he emerges from the wreckage having saved the world from destruction is a delightful vision of male shyness being conquered by the enthusiastic love of a nasal-voiced woman.

But somewhere in between the making of the first and second *Ghostbuster* films someone decided that Janine wasn't good enough for Egon. In fact, she should now go out with the weirdo accountant Louis – played, inevitably, by Rick Moranis – who not only was repeatedly turned down by Sigourney Weaver in the first film (in other words, set up as someone to be rejected by all but the very desperate) but, it was suggested in the final scene of the first film, possibly left deranged by his experience of being turned into a dog (it's a long story).

In fact, there is no reference at all to Egon and Janine's relationship in the second film; that moment on Central Park West meant, it seems, nothing. Instead, sexy Janine has to roll around on the sofa with weirdo Louis. Presumably the writers made this decision, and it just so happens that one of the co-writers of *Ghostbusters 2* was none other than … Harold Ramis. The heartless cad.

Needless to say, Sigourney Weaver, who plays the main love interest in the first *Ghostbuster* film, is still very much presented as the hot female in the second, despite being dull, not funny and a little bit whiny. She also, as it happens, has a breathy voice. Maybe THAT'S the secret: it's not that women have to be boring and not funny to attract men, they just have to talk on the heavy exhale.

This trope of the funny woman being sidelined in favour of the boring woman is part of another well-loved (by screenwriters) movie stereotype, the Funny Female Friend.

The Funny Female Friend is, by now, a well-known cliché in movies, especially romcoms, and TV shows, especially sitcoms. It is as tired as those other great stock movie characters, Magical Negro (as coined by Spike Lee, refers to a wise and sexless black character, usually played by Morgan Freeman); BBF, or Black Best Friend (noted by *LA Times* writer Greg Braxton in 2007, similar to Magical Negro, except the BBF is young and female and her 'principal function is to support the [young and white] heroine, often with sass, attitude and a keen insight into relationships and life',* so maybe she's Magical Negro's daughter) and Manic Pixie

---

* 'Buddy System', Greg Braxton, *LA Times*, 29 August 2007.

Dream Girl (coined in 2008 by Nathan Rabin of the AV Club: she's unconventional! But not scarily so! She is conceived purely to liven up a boring guy's boring life! And sometimes she dies or at least disappears before she and the wistful male protagonist actually get together so he never has to deal with all that unappetising relationship stuff, like menstruation and general humanity – see: *One Day*! Wheeeeee!), all of whom exist to assist the main character achieve his life or her goal. I'd quite like to see a movie starring just these characters. It would be like watching three car-less sat-navs barking instructions at one another, going pathetically nowhere.

The Funny Female Friend refers to, as you might have guessed from the name, the wisecracking female friend of the main character who is, generally, female but not necessarily and she's probably played by Joan Cusack.

And there's nothing wrong with any of that – except the Funny Female Friend is almost never allowed to have a love life of her own. She is there to help the main character with his or her love life and to provide witty insights about the other gender, but that's it. Because who would want to go out with a funny friend when the main female is so much less funny and therefore less threatening, right? A woman with a personality: good as a friend, not as a girlfriend. This is the only explanation for Hugh Grant rejecting sharp and funny Kristin Scott Thomas – KRISTIN SCOTT THOMAS – for dullsville and monotone Andie MacDowell – ANDIE MACDOWELL – in *Four Weddings and a Funeral*, even though MacDowell can't even comment on the rainy weather without sounding like she's slipping into a coma. Instead, poor Kristin ends up with Prince Charles. Jesus, Richard Curtis, why don't you just burn the witch at the stake?

There are occasional movies in which the Funny Female Friend is allowed to find true love. *When Harry Met Sally* is probably the best example of that, with Marie (Carrie Fisher) bagging Jess (Bruno Kirby) and living happily ever after with him and, briefly, his wagon wheel table, long before Harry (Billy Crystal) and Sally (Meg Ryan) get together. But that is possibly because that movie was written by Nora Ephron who, it is probably safe to say, was a very funny female friend.

When Harry Met Sally is the exception to this rule and many, many others, not least in giving the main female character an actual and appealing personality. In the main, the role of the Wisecracking Female Friend is there to make the main woman look even more bland in comparison which, according to movie logic, makes her even more feminine and desirable. So while this is a definitely depressing theory, it does at least resolve one of the great modern mysteries: Andie MacDowell's film career.

4. Women never talk to one another or, if they do, they only talk about men

In 1985 two women, Allison Bechdel and Liz Wallace, invented the Bechdel Test to ascertain the gender bias of a movie, something that is so easy to do that the test consists of only three questions:

1. Does the movie contain two or more female characters who have names?
2. Do these characters talk to each other?
3. Do they discuss something other than a man?

It is astonishing how many films fail this test. Not just the obvious ones, i.e. cop movies and chick flicks, but good ones!

Funny ones! Ones that you almost certainly love. Put it this way, *The Princess Bride* fails this test. *The Princess Bride*! Inconceivable!

Part of the problem here is that so many movies feature only one woman amid a group of men. Katha Pollitt dubbed this trope, brilliantly, the Smurfette Principle for reasons you can perhaps guess. *The Princess Bride*, for example, conforms to the Smurfette Principle, as do *Super 8*, *Inception* and *Star Wars*. In these movies, the women do not get a chance to prove that sometimes, amazingly, they do talk to one another about things other than the opposite sex because there are no other women for them to talk to.

But even when there is a secondary female part, she is usually just, as already discussed, the sassy sidekick, and the sassy sidekick is there to help the main character achieve her goals, and obviously the only goal that main woman could have is to be in a relationship.

Interestingly, this assumption that boys'n'break-ups are the only subjects women discuss when they're together is not limited to the silver screen. While I was writing this book – yes, this very book you're holding in your hand, how meta is this, eh? – I happened to go to a book party. Towards the end of the evening I got talking to a couple of (male) editors and agents and mentioned I was working on something aimed primarily at women (not that I'm being segregationist here). Their near unanimous response, was, 'Oh, are you writing a book about relationships?'

Turns out movies aren't the only medium to buy this line.

5. You have to give up your job to find happiness if you're a woman

There is an interesting dichotomy when it comes to a character quitting their job in a film. If a man does it at the beginning of the film, you are probably watching a horror movie, particularly if he then also moves his family to a big house in the country with only weirdos and a graveyard for neighbours.

If a woman does it in the middle or at the end of the movie, you are probably watching a romantic comedy. The female character then goes on to learn that she has been wasting her life with her totally skewed values about wanting to earn money and have self-respect and stuff, and is instead about to meet or has already met a guy who is probably something adorable like a vet or a coffee shop manager and who she can now get together with because he won't be threatened by her salary.

It's such a fabulously retro cliché I almost admire it, promoting the nigh-on 1950s theory that women only work until they get married, but with an added twist that any woman who dares to earn more than a man will spend her life wearing really terrible skirt suits and feeding her cat (not a metaphor).

To be fair, there is one film in which I do approve of a woman quitting her job at the end: *Pretty Woman*, as Vivian has quit the prostitute beat just before Richard Gere climbs up her fire escape (again, not a metaphor). Although seeing as prostitution is what brought them together, I don't think one can justly describe this as a feminist triumph or even a happy ending. And if you're making a pun about 'happy endings' in your head right now, I hope you're proud of yourself.

6. Falling in love and getting married are the only possible happy endings, especially for a woman

Here's another personal anecdote: a few years ago, I got it into my head that maybe I should write a novel. All you do is sit around and make stuff up, right? How hard can THAT be? (Very, it turned out.) I then spoke to an agent, who was and, as far as I know, still is a woman, about my idea. I wanted to write, I said, a book about a young woman who thought that the only important thing in life was to have a boyfriend and ends up in an unhappy relationship with a doofus because of this misguided belief. At the end, she finally learns the error of her ways and leaves him and gets a really fabulous, fulfilling job, the end.

There were at least two problems with this idea, and I saw one and the agent saw the other. The one I soon saw was that Curtis Sittenfeld had already written this book. It is called *The Man of My Dreams* and it is straight out fantastic and a billion times better than anything I would have written (this is not self-deprecation: this is a fact).

The agent saw a different problem: 'I just don't see that being happy with one's job is a happy ending,' she replied. 'Couldn't she have a male friend who she doesn't really notice in the book but gets together with at the end?'

And that really is a GREAT idea: a man in the background who the heroine doesn't notice but turns out to be perfect. So perfect, in fact, that Jane Austen (*Pride and Prejudice*, *Emma*, *Sense and Sensibility*) did it. And Shakespeare (*Much Ado About Nothing*). And every single chick lit author and romcom screenwriter in the world.

Personally, I reckon that finding a job that one loves is a happy development, or at least a much more satisfying one than slapping the reader in the face with an old cliché that they have read a million times before. I also think that a young woman learning that being in a relationship is not necessarily synonymous with – and certainly not the only synonym for – happiness is also a good thing. And if these things combine, well, isn't that a really happy ending?

Don't waste too much time considering the answer because the question is rhetorical as I decided, out of the benevolence of my heart, to spare the world and the novel was never written. But this exchange, as well as making me mildly concerned for the publishing world, made me think how few happy endings there are for female characters in movies, primarily, but also books, other than the romantic one. Is this down to a belief that marriage is the only REAL form of happiness for women and anything else is just compensation, or is it a dearth of imagination? Well, in the last chapter of this book I suggest the former. But what the heck, this book is a broad church, so let's say in this chapter it's the latter.

So to help both the publishing and movie industries, and maybe also that agent, here are some alternative happy endings:

> The character can't find her phone and because she has turned it off she couldn't locate it simply by ringing it. Yet eventually she finds it, in the fridge on top of the pickle jar. Cue power ballad!

> The character wakes up and it's a cold day. She puts on some tights and, amazingly, there is not a single hole in the first pair she tries on, not even at the big toe on the left foot where there is ALWAYS a hole. Triumph!

She boards a plane and not only is there not a
single baby in her cabin but the seat next to her
is empty. Heart-warming!

Her boss tells her that they're rearranging the
layout on her floor and she will now be by the
window and – at long last – far away from
Bella 'Bellow' Jameson and Mike the IT guy,
who everyone knows masturbates under his
desk. Inspiring!

She puts on her iPod and not one not two but
THREE Meat Loaf songs play in a row. Or is
that just too fantastical?

7. Women don't even consider having abortions …
any more

Look, I understand that a baby is a more obvious plot device
than a not-baby. I also get that pregnancy and childbirth
offer more potential for light-hearted comedy than an
abortion or, as Jonah Hill refers to it in *Knocked Up*, a
schmamortion. The reason Hill has to resort to the Yiddish
word for – gasp! – abortion is because that film, infamously,
presents it as something that is not just implausible, but
downright evil. When Alison (Katherine Heigl) – who has
just started a new dream job, is living in her sister's pool
house – gets pregnant after an awkward one-night stand with
a doofus, she doesn't even consider the option and other than
Hill, the only other character who suggests that she should
have an abortion is her mother. The mother is clearly
delineated as the boo-hiss villainess of this otherwise very
funny film when she follows up her advice to her daughter to

get it 'taken care of' by adding that later when she's married she can then have 'a real baby'.

As the title suggests, Alison does not have it 'taken care of' but rather has the baby – the real baby and gets together with the one-night stand doofus and they live happily ever after. Which is how all contraception-free, one-night stands end, kids.

As weird chance would have it, *Knocked Up* was one of three films, along with *Juno* and *Waitress*, that came out in 2007 that presented abortion as both unreasonable and unthinkable. It's highly unlikely any of these movies were intended as anti-abortion propaganda; instead they were the product of screenwriters who were part of a generation that had always had the luxury of relatively easy access to abortion and therefore had forgotten what the reality of the alternative is and, thus, sentimentalised it.

To be fair to these films, their entire plots depend on the character going through with the pregnancy so an abortion would have been not just a bit of a downer (although I would argue that an abortion is a lot less of a downer than having an unwanted child which ruins the mother's life and is therefore not given the maternal and pastoral care all babies deserve because its mother was simply not able to care for it properly, but carry on) but a film ender. Of course, the counter-argument to this is that perhaps the screenwriters should have come up with an idea that didn't depend on a woman behaving in a way that is completely unrealistic. An abortion is an operation and it is not a decision that any woman makes with a hop, skip and jump. But it is something that many women have had some personal experience with, either by having had one themselves or knowing someone who has done. And most women who are not politicians in the Republican Party or on the Christian right know that abortion is not an embodiment of evil that destroys potentially golden-lit happy families, but rather enables women to exert some control over their lives in a world in which people have sex and are not always as diligent as they should be about contraception. This is called living in the real world as opposed to madey-uppy Fairy Tale Romcom/ Republican Psycho World, and it's extraordinary how often those two worlds elide into one another (see also: the only happy ending for a woman is marriage; black people don't exist or, at least, aren't relevant; everyone is upper middle class, etc.).

A far dafter example of this refusal to consider abortion is in the far dafter film *I Don't Know How She Does It*, a searing investigation into how working mothers hold it together and the answer turns out to be, 'Pretty easily – if they have a battalion of staff and a very understanding husband.'

In one particularly ridiculous and downright offensive scene Sarah Jessica Parker's character, Kate, talks a young female colleague out of having an abortion, even though her pregnancy was unplanned, she does not appear to be in any kind of relationship and, as already inferred, she is planning to have an abortion. What's particularly weird about this moment in the movie is that in the original book version of it this colleague is in her late thirties and it therefore makes a little more sense why she would choose to go through with the pregnancy. In the film, they (inevitably) make the character about ten years younger as well as far more career-oriented, which therefore only heaps ridiculous on top of implausible. The fact is, it is a lot harder to raise a child if you don't have a partner and a household of staff, as Parker's character does. Moreover, this character's decision to have a baby is in no way essential to the plot so there is even less justification for sticking it in.

What's so particularly weird about Hollywood's aversion to even discussing abortion is that this was not always the case. While I can't, thankfully, think of a movie that treats abortion as a laff-a-minute, there are plenty of films made just a few decades ago in which a character has an abortion and this is treated as neither gloomy nor evil, nor even so momentous that it needs to be central to the film. Amid all the spaghetti arms and watermelons, *Dirty Dancing* (1987) smuggles in a little side plot about the importance of legal and available abortions.* The only person in this plot who is portrayed as evil is not the woman who considers and – gasp – has the abortion, but the jerk who abandons her. This is also true of *Fast Ties at Ridgemont High* (1982) in which poor Jennifer Jason Leigh isn't judged by the film for having sex – and underage, too – but the schmuck who not only gets her pregnant but then breaks his promise to drive her to the clinic very much is. Instead, her kindly older brother, played by Judge 'Where is he now' Reinhold picks her up, promises not to tell their parents and drives her home, proving his good guy credentials, while she is no worse for wear. In *High Fidelity* (2000), Rob (John Cusack) casually mentions that his now ex-girlfriend Laura had an abortion and while that

---

* Great teen movies in the eighties were particularly adept at sneaking in serious stuff beneath the sequinned topcoat. *Dirty Dancing* had the abortion plot; in *Say Anything*, Frasier's father (John Mahoney), or in this film, Diane Court's (Ione Skye) father, was imprisoned for tax violations; in *Pretty in Pink*, the father couldn't get over his wife leaving and the family was on the breadline. Even if most people don't recall these darker side plots when they think back on these films now, remembering instead Molly Ringwald's unbelievably awful prom dress in *Pretty in Pink*, these side plots were what gave the films heft.

wasn't the reason the relationship foundered, his immaturity, as epitomised by his reaction to the abortion, eventually destroyed the relationship.

This suggests that either Hollywood is getting more conservative or it thinks audiences are. Maybe both. But whatever is changing, one thing that is not – despite the best efforts of right-wing politicians and fear-mongers – is that women in most western countries still have a choice. One day, maybe screenwriters, directors, actors and especially actresses, instead of making token platitudes in interviews about how great it is that women have 'a choice' these days, will insist on making movies that reflect just that.

8. A woman's personality is revealed through her eating habits. Also, thin women eat tonnes and never put on weight

Considering how Hollywood is repulsed by fat women, it sure does love to show the ladies chowing down, and, boy, does it make the chowing down symbolic. Take two movies which depicted women who were a little ambivalent about the whole wedding thing but were obsessed with food: *My Best Friend's Wedding* and *Bridesmaids*. Indeed, the female leads in these films based their entire careers around food being, respectively, a food critic and a pastry chef. And not only are these their jobs, they are, apparently, these women's personalities as Julia Roberts (the decidedly unlikely restaurant critic) and Kristen Wiig (the equally unlikely pastry chef) talk constantly about food and are shown eating it, fussing over it and, in the latter's case, expressing love through it. If either of these characters had any body fat, they would be portrayed as tragic podgemeisters with food addiction problems and en route to starring in the sequel to

What's Eating Gilbert Grape? As they don't, their interest in food and, in the case of *Bridesmaids*, ability to cook it is, I suspect, there solely to render them reassuringly feminine despite their antipathy towards marriage.

Conversely – and this is a bit of a cheat here, I know – the two characters who truly epitomise this cliché of a (gorgeous, thin) compulsive-eating ugly spinster whose personalities are summed up by their eating habits are not in the movies but on TV: *Ally McBeal* and Liz Lemon from *30 Rock*.

Clearly *30 Rock* is a much, much better show than *Ally McBeal* but Liz is little more than an updated Ally: great at her job, hopeless in love and at life in general, and, most of all, a veritable dump truck when it comes to eating. Liz (Tina Fey) and other characters talk endlessly about how much disgusting food this allegedly hopeless and homely woman eats. Ally McBeal (Calista Flockhart) banged on so much about cappuccinos and ice cream that show should have been sponsored by Haagen Dazs coffee-flavoured ice cream.

Yet in both cases, the actresses who play these characters are clearly gorgeous and slim (notoriously so, in Flockhart's case) and, more to the point, in neither case was eating a lot of food central to the show, except in the intimation that a woman eating is seen as synonymous with Loserhood and Spinsterville. Both these shows, incidentally, featured Jane Krakowski (playing, even more incidentally, the same part – the bubbly daft blonde). So maybe it was all her fault.

The messages are different between these examples – eating in *Bridesmaids* and *My Best Friend's Wedding* = feminine; eating in *30 Rock* and *Ally McBeal* = loser, sexual frustration – but the overall point is the same: a woman's relationship with food is so fraught with various frissons that not only is her personality conveyed through it but it can be made into a running gag. A woman who eats clearly has some kind of issues.

Another reason that movies love to show actresses eating is in the belief that this somehow makes the gorgeous, Amazonian woman on screen more relatable to audience members, even if the actresses themselves remain, of course, as thin as ever. Thus, they are fuckable in the eyes of male audiences and relatable in the eyes of female audience members. Win win!

For all the criticisms one can make about the Bridget Jones films – namely, the way the story was boiled down to focus purely on Bridget's love life – at least Renée Zellweger did bulk herself up enough so that she did, actually, look, if not fat, then curvy enough to seem like a credible thirty-two-year-old woman who ate junk and drank a lot of white wine.

When I see Charlize Theron chowing down junk food in *Young Adult*, or Cameron Diaz doing the same in *Bad Teacher* I don't think, Wow, I can totes relate to her! I'm going to come back and see every single performance of this film! She is SO me. I think, I am incredibly insulted that filmmakers think that making the character eat like a John Belushi with the munchies will make me relate to her. And I'm also incredibly insulted that they think I'm so dumb that I won't notice that, despite the constant caloric intake, she remains about as obese as a rake with an aerobics habit. Why do movie (and TV) studios patronise me and think I'm so stupid?

And then I eat a tub of ice cream while pondering the hopelessness of my life as *Vogue* calls and begs me to be its cover model.

9. Jewish men are smoking hot, Jewish women are non-existent and/or awful

Of all the things that have been said about Jewish men in the movies – Funny! Sweet! Smart! And with such adorably curly hair! – one quality has been intriguingly overlooked: they have amazing PR. This, of course, is because it is the filmmakers themselves who are doing the PR, yet the message they send is bizarrely one-sided and, speaking as a Jewish woman, goddamn wrong.

Spearheaded most famously by that uber-Jewish man PR mastermind, Woody Allen, along with his newly appointed baton holder, Judd Apatow, Jewish men in movies are almost invariably portrayed as funny, smart, geeky, funny, cute, funny, future high-earners, adorably dorky, hilariously neurotic, amusingly inclined towards hypochondria, articulate and funny (did I mention funny?). By contrast, I have yet to see a film in which, say, Natalie Portman or Scarlett Johansson's Judaism is portrayed as one of their main advantages, or even any advantage at all.* When Jennifer Grey was once asked why she felt the need to mutilate her glorious nose she replied, 'The thing is, Hollywood is run by Jewish men. We all know the Jewish syndrome in high school. The Jewish boys don't like the Jewish girls. They really want the goddesses and Michelle Pfeiffers.' That Grey's career went downhill after her

---

* Interestingly, the young woman who Woody Allen had a relationship with and about whom he wrote *Manhattan* was, according to various reports, Jewish in real life, but for the film he cast the decidedly blonde-haired, blue-eyed non-Semitic Mariel Hemingway in the role. Admittedly, of all the creepy elements to *Manhattan*, this one barely makes the top three (although I'd definitely put it in the top five), but, nonetheless, it's odd.

73

unfortunate nose job is, in my view, due more to poor rhinoplasty than flawed reasoning.

Because the fact is, Grey is right: onscreen, Jewish women are generally portrayed as spoilt, nagging, high-maintenance, screechy and well-endowed in the nasal department. Thus, the Jewish men go after non-Jewish, ideally blonde women and they attract these goy women by their allegedly innate Jewish qualities (funny, funny, funny!). One sees this in many movies beyond the Allen and Apatow oeuvres, such as *When Harry Met Sally* (Harry eats corned beef on rye, Sally eats turkey on white – how much more obvious a clue do you need?), *The Wedding Singer* and an awful lot of Ben Stiller films, as well as TV shows from *The OC* to *Curb Your Enthusiasm* to *Mad About You* to *Seinfeld*.

In fact, I can't remember a recent film in which the Jewish leading man pursues an obviously Jewish woman instead of the usual hot, thin and decidedly non-Jewish lady. Even in *Crossing Delancey*, an otherwise charming 1988 film about the matchmaking process between two Jewish thirty-somethings, the woman, Isabelle (played by the breathtakingly lovely Amy Irving) is notably less Jewish, in the strict sense, than Sam (the always appealing Peter Riegart). He sells pickles on New York's Lower East Side and is devout in his faith, she sleeps around with phoney European intellectuals and keeps a kitchen that most definitely doesn't look kosher. Ultimately, the message is the same: Jewish men are hot and they don't want Jewish women, who are either awful or invisible. Thus Jewish women find themselves in the same uncomfortable and unfair place as that of Asian men, in that the other gender of their demographic is portrayed as deeply desirable while they themselves are mocked or banished offscreen.

Seriously, Hollywood dudes, what happened to you guys in the past? Were you humiliatingly knocked back as teenagers by some sexy Jewesses at your Jewish summer camp and vowed to wreak revenge on the female of your species ever after? Or is this some kind of long-running retribution for Barbra Streisand's brilliant seduction of the most goy man ever on the planet, Robert Redford, in *The Way We Were*? Come back, Barbra, come back – your female people need you now.

In a 2009 essay in the *Tablet** Liel Liebovitz very smartly locates this stereotype to the origins of American cinema and burlesque, citing first the Minsky Brothers who only put blonde and red-haired non-Jewish women in their influential burlesque shows at the beginning of the twentieth century. While this decision on the part of the Minskys did spare Jewish women the indignities of shaking their tail feathers about for a roomful of slavering bootleggers and general nogoodniks, it also established the distinctly goyish template for female beauty for being 'exclusively yellow- or red-haired, cute and perky, never dark, never familiar'. Liebovitz then traces this tendency through the rise of Jews working in Hollywood in the twenties, thirties and forties and up to today's movie and TV industries. After all, one of the more beloved romantic plots for screenwriters today is, as Liebovitz says, for 'the non-Jewish woman – a goddess, after all – to extricate her Jewish lover from his suffocating, crass, and unhealthy environment and introduce him to her clean, well-lit world'.

Well, I'm calling bullshit on this. For a start, Jewish women have 'clean, well-lit worlds' too, you know. Hell, we have to

---

* 'Gentlemen Prefer Blondes', Liel Liebovitz, *Tablet*, 20 October 2009.

keep our flats extra tidy, us 'dark, familiar' Jewish ladies, what with our wiry, dark body hair moulting all over the place. Amirite or amirite?

Oh forget it – this trope is so stupid and universally offensive it doesn't even deserve sarcasm. It's offensive to Jewish women for obvious reasons. It's offensive to non-Jewish women for suggesting that they are all charming flibbertijibbets, like stand-ins from a regional theatrical version of *Along Came Polly*, who long to be introduced to the exciting world of matzos ball soup and will make tinkling laughs when their husband drops a random Yiddish word, ideally one beginning with that hilariously ethnic letter combination of 'schm'. And finally, despite what these filmmakers seem to think, it's offensive to Jewish men, suggesting that they all buy into an idea of assimilation and salvation so shallow it would have put their ancestors in the shtetl to shame.

Love knows no bounds and obviously I'm not arguing that Jewish men in movies should restrict their hearts to beating for those of the same faith. But for (the Old Testament) God's sake, let's have a bit of equality here and admit Jewish women are at least as hot as their male counterparts. We're funny, we're smart, we're neurotic – we're all that and more, with longer hair, softer skin and less chance of being named 'Moishe'. But if the Jewish men onscreen are too busy chasing after platinum shiksas to appreciate this, then let's see some Jewesses onscreen being frantically pursued by various blond men. Although not Matthew McConaughey, please. Come on, we Jews have suffered enough.

What to expect when your friends are expecting

Congratulations! Your friends have shagged. Now they're going to have a little sleep-depriving, bank-account-emptying bundle of joy and it's time to prepare yourself for the drastic life change you're about to experience, although admittedly not as drastic as that of your friends (thank God). For some reason, while there are millions of guides out there for expectant parents, there is, outrageously, nothing for the poor, confused, panicky friends of these baby-makers. At last this baffling oversight will be rectified. So put your feet up, set up a personal account at Le Petit Bateau and get ready to hear the unpastel-coloured truth.

As soon as the pregnancy has been announced you will learn, in the most extraordinary degree of detail, tales of your friends' sex lives. It is traditional that when a woman tells her girlfriends she is pregnant she must then describe for how long she and her partner were 'trying for a baby'. This is a pregnancy euphemism for 'having lots of joyless, stressful sex', and you should appreciate this euphemism as pretty much every other detail you hear will be related in bloodied detail. Some people are then privileged to hear where exactly the baby was conceived, a revelation that can feel a little disconcerting if, say, it happened to be on a holiday on which you accompanied them. In short, be prepared to feel like a teenager who has just caught her parents having sex.

On one level, of course you know your friends have sex – you might have even discussed it at times with at least one of them. But now you are expected to talk about it in some dreadful, po-faced 'creation-of-life' way as opposed to the way it should be discussed by adults: giggly and drunkenly. Already your life is changing so much.

Handy hint! If both the parents of the baby-to-be are present during the retelling of the conception, try not to think about how this is like a deeply unerotic live version of a sex line which people phone to hear stories about other people's sex lives. Instead, just nod solemnly and replay the plot of *The Shawshank Redemption* in your head to block out the noise but simultaneously achieve that requisite serious-but-uplifted facial expression.

So now that your mind has been filled with images of your friends anxiously rutting away, it is time to learn more about the results of said rutting. In truth, the pregnancy will likely be the relatively easy stage for you as it will feel like your friend has a very long cold in that she tires easily, is off alcohol and occasionally looks a bit green. So all in all, pretty painless for you. Until the last month.

This is called the Gross Out Stage as you will now be forced to hear all sorts of medical, biological and gynaecological details that you are strongly urged to block out if you have even the slightest thought that you might like to have a baby yourself one day. On the one hand, she is being a good friend by telling the Truth about this whole pregnancy thing so you are spared the surprises she has endured, as well as acting as a kindly corrective to the romanticised idea that pregnancy is a beautiful stage of life. On the other hand, it would be nice if those lessons didn't involve her telling you how many doctors have stuck their fingers up her that day. You see, by this point she will be so desperate to get this baby out, so accustomed to her body being treated by doctors as little more than a baby pod, that she will forget that others are not quite as let-it-all-out (so to speak) about what's going on inside her vagina. So just as she has been told to do pelvic exercises throughout her pregnancy, as her friend you are advised to do ear blocking exercises, tightening and releasing the muscles in your ear canals to prevent any information getting through and lodging in your brain FOR EVER.

As the due date approaches and, most likely, is bypassed with no child emerging, your friend will be extremely uncomfortable and understandably desirous of others sharing her pain. She will do this by grossing out everyone around with liberal use of the following words and phrases:

- ✴ 'mucus plug'
- ★ 'discharge'
- ✴ 'leakage'
- ✴ 'wind'
- ★ 'lactate'
- ✴ 'dilate'
- ✴ 'speculum'
- ★ 'vaginal wall'
- ✴ 'look, you can see his hand pushing out against my stomach'
- ✴ 'literally sitting on my bladder'

Tighten and release those ear canal muscles. Tighten. Release. And then tighten again. Hard.

Handy hint! When your friend talks about having 'a sweep', do not then visualise Dick van Dyke in his cheeky chappy chimney sweeper outfit heading up into her uterus to do a rendition of 'Step in Time'. Laughter is the inappropriate response to your friend's news.

Just to confirm that pregnancy destroys any connection sex might have to love and desire, your friend is likely to talk about how she now 'makes' her partner have sex with her in the hope it will trigger childbirth. When she relates this to you, simply nod and say what a good idea that is. Do not say, 'You mean you're using a penis to smoke out the baby?'

Throughout the pregnancy, you are likely to hear long discussions about whether or not your friend will have her baby at home or in hospital, and there may be a strong undercurrent of anxiety and defensiveness to these speeches, no matter how certain she is. Do not, under any circumstances, come over all Judgey McJudge here and express doubt in her choice, nor email her articles advocating either method. Chances are your friend has, between her seventeenth and eighteenth trip to the loo in a single night, researched the matter fully on the internet and her head is so full of bloggers and columnists talking crap on the matter by this point that your input will be as welcome as a gatecrasher at a small and somewhat heated family dinner. No matter how welcoming the hostess appears to be, no matter how much input she asked from you in planning the menu, you are not supposed to be there. Moreover, unless you have an extraordinarily homogenous group of friends, different ones will make different choices about how to give birth so don't stick your flag in either camp. Unless anyone expresses plans to give birth in the middle of a motorway, just nod and ask for the address to send the flowers.

She's had the baby! And what a lovely little cherub has improbably emerged from her insides. Now, if you think you had heard all there was to hear about your friend's body by this stage, prepare to lose your innocence. To use a sex analogy (and why not? We've already talked about medical fingering), heretofore you've only been making out. Prepare for hardcore S & M. Possibly because your friend cannot believe what her body has proven capable of doing, she will then feel the need to describe the childbirth in varying amounts of detail. Here are some more words that you will now have to endure:

★ 'tearing'
✶ 'ripping'
✶ 'stitches'
★ 'splitting in half'
✶ 'crowning'
✶ 'that means when the head starts to come out'
★ 'literally, we could see the head coming out'
✶ 'but the shoulders were the worst. They were what caused the tearing'
✶ 'enema'
★ 'shitting all over the table'

Hopefully by now you will have been doing your ear blocking exercises and your canal muscles will not let through a single syllable. If not, you have only yourself to blame for your slack muscles and ensuing mental trauma.

Handy hint! If your friend or her husband offer to show you photos over lunch of how much she 'dilated' and the moment when the head first emerged, unless you enjoy looking at a stretched-out vagina while eating a sandwich, say no, no and thrice no. And then maybe don't see those friends again for a while.

For the first few months you will be in the infant stage. It can come as something of a shock to go over to what was once your friend's lovely, peaceful flat where you've had many chatty cups of tea and many ranting glasses of wine and find a strange mewling creature, covered in babysick, crying in inexpressible confusion, living only from feeding to feeding, nap to nap, and that's just your friend. Of course, different friends have different needs in the first few months of their child's life. Some are desperate for some sign of life beyond the crib and the commandments of Gina Ford. Others can't even remember how to brush their hair. You know your friend so, sod Gina Ford: trust your instincts and act accordingly.

Although babies are notoriously expensive for the parents, they work out as quite handy little money savers for the parents' friends. You might look at the amount you spend on Le Petit Bateau onesies and marvel that not only did you not spend that money on your person but not even on a child who emerged from your person, but that is to take a short-term view. When your friends reproduce, they will then not be able to go out without the expenditure of at least £50 before they leave their front door and military planning. This is boring for them and it is also extremely boring for you to hear about every time you suggest an outing. (Some people find the 'no drinking during pregnancy and breast-feeding' to be the most tedious part of their friends becoming parents; those who know better say having to hear constantly about childcare arrangements is really the killer for which to prepare yourself.) To save all of you the bother, you will hereon socialise almost entirely with them at their houses and drink wine – VERY QUIETLY – in their front room. This might sound like a bit of a downer but, think of it this way: over a period of, say, five years, taking into account all the taxis into town you won't pay for, all the overpriced cocktails you will no longer buy in bars, all the clothes and shoes that you won't buy for going out, all the phone calls you won't make apologising for your behaviour the night before, you will save roughly a million pounds. (Note: this money-saving benefit will disappear when your friends then move out to the suburbs-for-the-space – outer space, more like – which will entail you spending about £75 just to get to their house from the station in sodding Teddington.) If, as often happens, a bunch of your friends have babies at the same time, you will spend every Saturday afternoon for the next five months going house to house like a country doctor, expressing admiration over each (identical) baby, hearing (identical) tales of sleeplessness and nursery strife, seeing (identical) piles of bouncy baby chairs and Maisy Mouse books. Should the visits all begin to meld into one another and you find yourself struggling to remember where you are and how to get home, simply follow the path of Petit Bateau boxes and Baby Gap bags that you have trailed in your wake as you have gone from house to house, like Hansel and Gretel's path of crumbs but with fewer carbohydrates and more pastel.

Remember, because your babied-up friends are now being held under house arrest by a small tyrant who has invaded their home they are completely ignorant of anything going on in the real world, i.e. what's on at the cinema, what's in *Grazia* that week, any music that has been released in the past year, gossip about other friends, etc. So you might feel that it is your duty to relay to them all these details, like Anne Sullivan translating the outside world to the deaf and blind Helen Keller, breaking through their isolation. But bear in mind that your friends are likely to prove even more impermeable to these lessons than Helen.

Handy hint! Don't even bother to ask any question that begins with 'Have you seen …' unless the end of that sentence is '… Peppa Pig?' or '… where the burping blanket is?'

After about a year, you should have settled into some sort of routine, one that generally involves you becoming very au fait with the napping and feeding schedules of your friends' children and working your life around them accordingly. You will become so indoctrinated with the thought that ringing a doorbell will lead to chaos – aka, waking up the baby – that you will find yourself texting your parents when you are outside their front door, even though the last baby they had in their house was, in fact, you. Any socialising you do in the outside world with your friend-turned-mother will mainly be spent looking for a café that is child friendly with aisles wide enough to accommodate a small aircraft or a Bugaboo, whichever is wider.

Obviously, you love all your friends' children (well, most of them.). You cannot believe that this tiny being has emerged from your friend's loins and what a marvellous combination it is of her and her partner's genetics. You are filled with awe at how your friend manages to do this whole parenting thing when you can't even keep a pot plant alive for more than a week. It really is quite incredible. And you are, of course, very, very happy for them.

But.

There may come a point when you find it all, well, a bit dull. Other people's babies are lovely but they are somewhat interchangeable: small, squishy and with a tendency to cry or hit things at crucial points in a conversation. As you felt like a silly teenager during the pregnancy, shocked by hearing about your friend's sex life and then grossed out by the overly described results of sex life, you may now find yourself feeling a little like an eight-year-old child who has just been presented with a younger sibling: no longer can you rely on the full attention of your friends.

Now, as these people are your friends, presumably they are not total dicks who will talk to you as if their lives are inherently superior to your life simply because they didn't use contraception one night. If they do, obviously these people should immediately lose the privilege of your company.

But even non-dickish new parents will be so consumed with a concern to which you cannot quite connect. Some friends might disappear completely into a soupy fog of parenting for the next eighteen years, too stressed to think about anything other than their child. More commonly your friends will try to hold on to some shreds of their pre-baby persons, but even they, despite themselves, will be inevitably submerged in the Sea of Parenting.

Whatever conversation you have with them from here on, you will notice that their eyes frequently dart elsewhere and there is a slightly glazed tone in their voices, one that suggests a disconnect between thought and words. While the words may be saying, 'Oh, that is fascinating, please tell me about your latest office crush,' their thoughts will be, Oh my God, has he swallowed a pound coin?! Has he stuck his fingers in a plug socket?! Has he been kidnapped by ETA?!?! Simultaneously, you'll hear yourself talking about the latest chaos in your life and your heart will sink at what a cliché you sound – the messy childless friend! Ho ho! – and you know, too, how silly your concerns compared to your friend's constant vigilance to keep a small person from injuring themselves. Yet they are still your concerns, and they once were your friend's, too.

Whereas once you could rely on 100 per cent of your friend's attention, you are now lucky to get, at most, 20 per cent. It's like when they first get together with a new love, but without the security that they will be back to normal in a matter of weeks. Your friend will never, really, be back to how they once were.

They will take longer to phone you back, spontaneity will have gone the way of the dodo bird and they will be especially hard to track down on the days you used to see them the most: the weekends. That is no longer drinking time. That is family time. No more holidays together, no more carefree nights out without worrying about the babysitter. At least, not for a while.

Seeing a bunch of your friends all having babies at the same time can bring up all sorts of unexpected anxiety that you don't have a child, especially if you assumed you'd have one, too, by this age. You might also feel brutally excluded when they all start bandying words about together like 'NCT group' and 'nursery waiting lists' that mean absolutely nothing to you and you can only sit there, waiting, thinking about how this is just like when they all really got into Sonic Youth in the sixth form while you were still dancing to

George Michael. Then there's the horror of watching you and your friends adhere to your clichéd roles, you slightly resenting that you don't get your friend to yourself any more but pretending you don't, her speaking wistfully about your carefree single life when actually you spent last night alone eating rice pudding in your bathrobe while watching *Poirot*.

Of course you are supportive of your friend and want to help her as much as you can during this huge upheaval in her life. And you know that this is not the time for an episode of The Me Show: it is your friend's time, your friend's time to figure out how on earth she is going to do this whole motherhood thing and it's your job as a friend to cheer her on. But privately, it can feel unsettling, boring, occasionally irritating, even lonely and a little bit sad, if not quite the death of something, then certainly the shifting. Obviously you cannot say any of this – especially to your newly babied up friends – as you will sound, well, like a self-obsessed spoilt eight-year-old child who has just been presented with a new sibling, and they are all-consumed with other issues, anyway. But it's inevitable and normal, both your friend's change and your reaction, and it's something that just is. Be careful not to take these feelings out on her, or even really talk them through with her as, however good a friend she is, she will not really be able to understand and will probably feel a little attacked. Don't start resenting women with babies out of jealousy or loneliness as that is the fast track to self-loathing. Instead talk your feelings through with your baby-free friends.

The obvious solution is simply to spend more time with your baby-free friends but life is not simple. For a start, friends are not like bars of soap that you simply replace and swap round. Different friends have different qualities and offer different things. Second, as mentioned before, it is often the case that a whole slew of friends have babies at the same time, making any possible swapping even trickier and, speaking frankly, exacerbating the aforementioned loneliness. Not only have your friends changed but your social life has inexorably changed while you, unlike your friends, have not. It's not easy, but it is, honestly, only temporary. It is at this point that you might start thinking about getting a pet.

Handy hint! When your friend's otherwise adorable child shouts for his mother for the third time when you are talking about bumping into your ex-boyfriend with his new girlfriend, envisage how much you're going to embarrass this kid at his sixteenth birthday by talking about the time he projectile-pooed when he was three months old and managed to clog up his dad's laptop from a distance of six feet.

When this funny little thing that has somehow emerged from your friend starts walking and talking and having its own very distinct personality, the fun for you truly begins. There is no better way to tease your friend than using their child to do so.

Recommended games to play with your friend's child:

* Tell them the name your friend was known by at university and get them to use it instead of Mummy.
* Teach them songs about poopoo, peepee and – snigger – diarrhoea that they will sing, on loop, non-stop, for the next three years.
* Teach them vaguely naughty and extremely irritating words like 'durrh-brain' and 'duh!'

* Tell them to ask your friend questions like, 'Mummy, what really DID happen between you and Robbie Damigo that night after A-levels at Christina's house?'
* Teach them the dance moves to Whigfield's 'Saturday Night'.

You will be amazed at how much fun all the above are.

Hopefully by now you should feel fully equipped for what is to come and by the time you're teaching the little tyke the Baseball Diarrhoea song (consult 1980s slushfest film *Parenthood* for further elaboration), you'll know you're doing just fine.

Look, this is not an easy life change you're about to go through, so don't beat yourself up if you ever find yourself wanting to stand in the middle of Baby Gap and scream, 'How the hell do I know if he's big or small for his age? Just give me a fucking onesie, OK?'

But ultimately, it is a wonderful one too. Your friend is having a baby! This means, if you like babies, you can now go round and play with it whenever you like without having to do the 3 a.m. feeding or bottom wiping. It's like rent-a-baby, with you enjoying all the good and none of the exhausting and disgusting.

And if you don't like babies, seeing how unbelievably tired your friend is every time you pop round and then backing away in horror as you notice a dollop of baby poo hanging off the cuff of her bathrobe will only serve to vindicate your decision. This is what we call a win-win situation, for both you and your friend.

Handy hint! When your friends then have their second baby, accept that you will probably not hear from them for at least the next five years.

Talking about eating disorders without using a single photo of Kate Moss

You know what's so brilliant about eating disorders? They're just so goddamn photogenic!

After all, they

1. mainly involve women and – even better – girls who
2. have a whiff of tragedy about them (few things better than a tragic female);
3. are caused by celebrities and fashion models;
4. involve, centrally, a female body, which is already exciting but, on top of that, this female body tends to change its shape quite drastically because of the illness (one of the aforementioned few things that is better than a tragic female is a female body that very visibly changes shape) and
5. feature food that is eaten or, in this case, not eaten to obtain that shape;
6. can be illustrated with a photo of Kate Moss who is, of course, the cause of all eating disorders.

With such a catalogue of attributes it is no surprise that the media love a good eating disorder story. In fact, it's hard to think of a single other subject that combines so many pieces of media catnip. Not even an A-level success story that can be illustrated with blonde triplets jumping up and down in vest tops and denim miniskirts upon learning that they have made the grades for Cambridge can compete with a doozy of an anorexia tale.

Eating disorders receive what could almost be described as a touching amount of attention in the media – far more than any other mental illness, in fact. But that is because the media do not see eating disorders as a mental illness, mental illnesses generally being, after all, not very sexy. They see them as – well, let's have the tabloids themselves explain eating disorders. True, seeing as one cannot even trust the media to get the details of celebrities' love lives straight one might hesitate at taking tips about psychology from such publications. But given that they themselves feel so confident to sound off about them, at length, and at pretty much a weekly rate to millions of readers, their thoughts merit investigation.

According to someone in the *Sun* called 'Carol Cooper, *Sun* Doctor' (the medical honorifics are, presumably, invisible), eating disorders are born from 'images of extremely skinny people, talk of diets, talk of obesity … body image problems [and] the modern day couch potato lifestyle'.* One can only assume that space constraints prevented 'Dr' Cooper from chucking rap music, the liberal media bias and single mothers into that litany of causation.

---

* 'My View', Carol Cooper, *Sun*, 1 August 2011.

The *Daily Mail* has been a true grizzly mama in defending the tender, vulnerable minds of women (and it is only women who suffer from eating disorders in these publications, of course) against those evil beasts, 'ultra-slim celebrities'* and the fashion industry, such as in this interestingly headlined article: 'Skeletal Models and Super-sized Hypocrisy: as fashion models insist they've turned their backs on anorexic chic, do they think we're blind?'*2

There is no doubt the fashion industry has a relationship with female body shape that is, to use the technical term, 'fucked up'. But it is not alone in displaying 'super-sized hypocrisy' (and that food portion size reference in the headline is just ADORBS) about this subject.

There is a fascinating correlation between how vehemently a publication blames eating disorders on celebrities, the diet industry and fashion – and how much general discussion about women's bodies that publication itself engages in, daily.

Take, as an example of 'super-sized hypocrisy' and an assumption of blindness, the front page of the Mail Online when it splashed on the aforementioned story about the number of children now being treated for eating disorders and how the aforementioned 'ultra-slim celebrities' are to blame, proving the 'devastating impact of children's obsession with body image'. If fashion designers really do think 'we' are blind, then their belief would appear to be well-founded regarding the editors of the Mail Online seeing as, just inches away on that website's front page on which this story was splashed, was another story debating which female

---

* 'Anorexia Victims Aged Five: doctors blame ultra-slim celebrities as almost 100 under-9s are treated in hospital', *Daily Mail*, 1 August 2011.

*2 *Daily Mail*, 23 February 2011.

celebrity has 'the best bikini body'. Perhaps the person in charge of headlining stories about eating disorders in tabloid newspapers is kept locked in solitary confinement in the office broom cupboard, deprived of sunlight, literacy lessons and glimpses of their own newspaper. This would explain their oft-expressed horror at 'ultra-slim celebs' despite working for publications that obsess over female celebrities' bodies with the gimlet-eyed obsession of someone suffering, well, a mental illness, equating weight gain with moral failure* and the loss of weight after having a child as the greatest possible female accomplishment.*2,*3

The surest way for a C-list or even Z-list female celebrity to get the attention of these papers and magazines is, aside from being arrested or dating a B-list actor, to lose a truckload of weight. The less there is of a female celebrity to see, the more the tabloid press sees her. Nicole Richie launched an entire career of celebritydom from this base. Calista Flockhart, LeAnn Rimes, Jennifer Aniston and Kate Bosworth have also all received far more media coverage than

---

* 'Oprah blames weight gain on failure to find work/life balance', *Daily Mail*, 5 May 2009.

*2 This blindness might also explain the interesting contradiction between this newspaper's hysterical obsession with 'the sexualisation of children' (generally caused by pop stars, the internet and even school uniforms) and its fondness for publishing photos of underage girls with headlines such as 'She Grew Up Fast! *Modern Family*'s Ariel Winter, 14, is sophisticated beyond her years at Disney World Car's ride opening. Looked gorgeous!' and photos of teenagers and children in bikinis with Humbert Humbert-esque captions such as: 'Exhibitionists: Kylie (16) and Kendall (14) Kardashian display maturity and a lifestyle far beyond their years'. But let's focus on one obscene contradiction in the media at a time.

*3 'Gisele looks stunning … just TWO MONTHS after she gave birth', *Daily Mail*, 24 June 2010.

their underpowered careers deserved because of their body size. Thousands of models appear in fashion shows every year but it was Jodie Kidd who the British media made into a near household name in the nineties when she appeared with her visible hipbones. There is a very thin line between the media expressing horror, and the media indulging in prurient, compulsive, even envious fascination.

It would be deeply satisfying to suggest that these publications are so evil that they are trying to encourage eating disorders among their readers by publishing daily photos of skinny celebrities, alternately praising them for their skinniness and then berating them for causing eating disorders, so as to ensure there will always be another anorexia story around the corner that can be illustrated with a photo of Kate Moss and a young girl lifting up her vest top to measure her tummy.* But as is almost invariably the case with conspiracy theories, this would be crediting the perpetrators with far too much intelligence. Rather, presenting unrealistic images of women while simultaneously blaming unrealistic images of women for causing eating disorders is neither as self-fulfilling nor as hilariously self-contradictory as it might seem. Rather, both of these tropes work perfectly alongside one another, not because they have anything at all to do with eating disorders, but because they are both part of the media's tendency to reduce women to physical bodies, and nothing more.

In the media, a woman is hot, nubile and fuckable, or she is fat, dried-up and laughable. This is not just in regard to celebrities and politicians but victims. So if you ever get kidnapped, arrested or die in a plane crash, make sure that

* 'Anorexic at Five', *Sun*, 1 August 2011.

you are, at the very least, attractive and ideally young as otherwise your photo will not be published in newspapers publicising your plight, even in your own country's papers.

Women – particularly but by no means exclusively in the tabloids – are judged purely by their bodies and valued accordingly. As a message, this is at least as pernicious as the one that comes from the fashion magazines that the tabloids so abhor, a message that is, ultimately, 'You have to be thin to wear these clothes.' That is by no means a healthy or even an economically sensible message, but it isn't quite as flat-out evil as the tabloids' message to women which is, essentially, 'Unless you are slim, conventionally pretty, fecund and under thirty-five you are essentially worthless.'

The *Sun*'s infamous Page 3 models are, beneath their sticky-lipped smiles and heartbreakingly hopeful looks, an interesting repository of irony. For a start, there's the paper's defence of having naked teenage and twenty-something girls in what is allegedly a 'news' paper (and a 'family' one at that) which generally goes along the lines of 'the girls get paid for it',* which sounds a lot like a man justifying pimping out his little sister. Quite how this sits with the paper's frequent denouncing of 'porn', 'pervs' and 'the sexualisation of children' who are allegedly exposed to so much porn every day from music videos, the internet and – er – the media is hard to say. No it isn't – it sits impossibly.

So it was interesting to see the *Sun* wonder on its front page why women and little girls feel such pressure to torture their bodies into looking a certain way, if indeed that's actually what eating disorders are, at their heart, really about.

---

* '"I Prefer Bazookas to Burkas" – Julie Burchill Backs Our Page 3 Girls', *Sun*, 10 October 2008.

The editors of the *Sun* really only needed to turn to that newspaper's page three. Yes, Page 3 models have curves, but what the publications and people who make that tired argument fail to understand is that the message is the same, no matter what the women look like: all you are is your body, and that is how you will always be valued and judged. This, incidentally, is why the media's slavering obsession with the occasional actress who appears who wears more than a B cup bra, such as Christina Hendricks, is exactly the same as a fashion magazine venerating a bone-thin model. Focusing on someone's figure is the same as reducing them to nothing more than their physique.

Moreover, by saying that eating disorders are simply caused by women wanting to look like the models and celebrities (who are otherwise praised in the same papers for being thin, but never mind), the media are reducing a serious mental illness – anorexia has the highest mortality rate of any mental illness – to being about nothing more than a woman's body, and her silly-billy obsession with it (which is, of course, nothing like these papers' obsession with women's bodies). Because that, in the eyes of the media, is all there is to a woman anyway.

It is a neat way of suggesting that women are so childlike and vulnerable that they need to be protected from too many photos of Renée Zellweger (in between Bridget Jones movies, of course) or else they'll go home and just take that dieting lark a bit too far.

It also allows these tabloids to wrench in their frequently expressed abhorrence of fashion magazines, an abhorrence that is only partly based on false outrage enabling them to pass the buck for what causes eating disorders. Fashion magazines, as you might have noticed and as I might have mentioned, fetishise skinniness. Tabloids fetishise the more conventional attributes of prettiness, ones that are associated with fertility (youth, breasts) and sex appeal (the aforementioned plus prettiness and good hair). This is because to the tabloids, women exist solely to appeal to men and have babies, and while I don't want to defend fashion's view of women's bodies, there is something interesting about an industry – one entirely geared to women, mind – that is completely uninterested in a woman's sex appeal. Women's fashion is not interested in making women look pretty and fecund. It is not interested in appealing to men at all; it's about impressing other women, whether that be with striking clothing, ridiculous shoes and – yes to a significant extent – self-denial. And this is why it drives the tabloids absolutely demented.

Any woman who appears to be doing something other than focusing 24/7 on getting married, having kids and attempting to clone themselves into Jools Oliver is seen as deeply, deeply suspect by huge swathes of the media, the *Daily Mail* and *Daily Telegraph* in particular. One sees this in their treatment of women who work and one definitely sees this in their attitude to female celebrities who remain bafflingly unmarried and childless over the age of thirty. So any magazine that appears to promote something other than the Tana Ramsayian way of life for women – i.e. fashion magazines – is treated by the tabloids with the kind of sniggering scorn and tutting horror others might reserve for an extreme fetish publication.

Thus, the way the media cover eating disorders manages the frankly multiskilled (I Don't Know How They Do It!) feat of making women sound infantile, body-obsessed and with nothing to offer other than their physical appearances, all the while allowing the papers themselves to affect high moral outrage and sneer at magazines while simultaneously publishing pictures of famous pretty women and skinny models from the hated fashion magazines. Frankly, they almost deserve a Pulitzer for the brilliance of their wheeze.

The oft-overlooked fact that 10 per cent of anorexics in the UK are men gets notably little coverage because a) thin men aren't quite as attractively vulnerable-looking as thin women and b) even the most blinkered tabloid editor knows that illustrating a story about a self-starving young man with a photo of Kate Moss would be pushing their luck. Also, the mere existence of male anorexia suggests that maybe Moss isn't actually to blame for anorexia – and who wants to run a story on that? That would be like saying maybe video games don't lead to violence, or smoking weed doesn't necessarily lead to heroin addiction. If it's not a story about tidy causation, it's a non-story.

It's not just the generalised coverage of eating disorders in the British media that is, to say the least, problematic, but the personalised, too.

It's quite a feat to present eating disorders in a more banal manner than the media already do, but that is what a certain journalist in a certain British tabloid manages to achieve.

This journalist – who shall be known here as Jiz Lones – frequently writes about her experiences with an eating disorder. Lones can take the most varied of subjects – recreational drugs,* colonics*2 – and turn them into a discussion about herself and her anorexia.

Now, even if she wrote about her illness in an honest,

---

* 'Meow Meow or Anorexia: if you're a teen who wants to rebel, you will', Liz Jones, *Daily Mail*, 22 March 2010.

*2 'The Ultimate Cleanse', Liz Jones, *Daily Mail*, 30 March 2011.

myth-dispelling, mature manner this would be, for Lones, worrying as it would suggest that her eating disorder is, in her eyes, her apparent primary self-identification. But it wouldn't necessarily be a bad thing in general as it could potentially educate people about what is still largely (but not solely) a woman's problem through a newspaper that has always been aimed at women but now, judging by its overall content, seems to have taken that brief and stuck an 'insulting' in between 'at' and 'women'. And, very occasionally, she does come close to doing this.

But, sadly, in the vast, vast majority of her articles, she does not.

Instead, she seems to depict her eating disorder as an odd little quirk for others to rubberneck;* something for which she seems happy to submit to public humiliation;*2 something that she almost appears proud of,*3 that she insists stemmed simply from a desire to resemble models in magazines*4 and that it is yet another aspect of her frequently vaunted self-obsession, along with her reliance on beauty products, fondness for facelifts and addiction to shopping. In my view, she has, sadly, for her sake and that of her readers, allowed herself to be made into an anorexic

---

* 'Fatten Me Up! What happened when I had to eat normally for three weeks?', Liz Jones, *Daily Mail*, 8 June 2009.

*2 See aforementioned colonic article – or, you know, don't.

*3 'I love my concave stomach and I can't help, despite my beliefs, but regard women who are fat, who don't exercise, who gorge on things like Galaxy, as somehow lazy. They just don't try hard enough', *Daily Mail*, 8 June 2009.

*4 'We're proof that glossy magazines CAN give you anorexia', *Daily Mail*, 4 May 2012.

minstrel, enacting the most inane and self-demeaning clichés about the illness: that it's something that afflicts attention-seeking women with too much time on their hands, who have an immature obsession with fashion magazines and celebrities, and who can only ever think, talk and write about themselves.

Lones's articles do as little to further the understanding of mental illness as the British tabloid that once described a celebrity who was suffering from a mental breakdown and had been admitted to a psychiatric hospital as a 'bonkers' 'nut' who was, nigh on Victorian-ishly, 'locked up'.*

But as morally indefensible as the latter example was, at least it was open about its beliefs and intentions: that people suffering from mental illness are dangerous and worthy targets of mockery.

Lones's articles are – whether she realises it or, more likely, not – more hypocritical because they are published with apparent intention of taking away the stigma of eating disorders while, it seems to me, only reinforcing them. The fault here clearly lies at least as much with the paper that publishes these pieces and encourages Lones to write them as with Lones herself, and, of course, that paper is the *Daily Mail*, a publication that is to women's mental wellbeing what Fox News is to reasoned political debate.

At the risk of deflating this massive media hard-on for eating disorders, this idea that skinny celebrities cause anorexia, and that anorexics are silly women who inhaled too much smoke from their Diptyque candles and lost all sense of perspective is perhaps not quite as true as some would like it to be.

---

* 'Bonkers Bruno Locked Up', *Sun*, 23 September 2003.

I make this claim without, admittedly, possessing a single medical qualification. But I am, perhaps, relatively more qualified than most who write on the subject.

There are plenty of memoirs out there from people who've had eating disorders and I have absolutely no interest in contributing to that pile, mainly because I feel that such things are only of interest to prurient voyeurs and people currently suffering from the illness who are looking for narcissistic companionship and validation. I am also extremely wary of appearing to do the same as Lones, reducing myself to Me and My Illness. So I'll just say that I was hospitalised when I was fourteen for severe anorexia nervosa and spent the next three or so years in various psychiatric hospitals. I did not look like Kate Moss: I looked, my mother said, like someone from Belsen, which seemed more appropriate for a Jewish girl than a supermodel. In fact, I doubt if I was even aware of Kate Moss's existence until several years after I first got ill as I was more interested in *Home and Away* and *Neighbours* than supermodels back then, fourteen and all. So maybe Erinsborough causes anorexia? Or Alf Stewart? Anyway, there you go: at least one anorexic whose illness was definitely not caused by Kate Moss.

I lost a lot of important years in hospital and even after I finally left for good, I lost more time to my two full-time jobs: being anorexic and trying to cover up being anorexic. It was a long time before I admitted it even to my closest friends who I made after hospitalisation (although the female friends had usually guessed and remained tactfully quiet; my male friends, sweetly, were completely stunned. The one gender generalisation I will allow is that women are better at perceiving signs of an eating disorder than men).

Many of the people I was in hospital with have since died, some from starvation, some from ensuing health complications, some from suicide. I was luckier. Eventually, I made a recovery of sorts and fear of food no longer dictates my daily life. But some experiences leave impermeable scars and that's just the way it is.

I don't believe personal experience imbues one with expertise. Nor is this a part of my life that I particularly enjoy discussing. In fact, I try to avoid talking about it altogether, mainly because I hope that I have something more to offer than my history. After working so hard to recover, I'd rather not spend the rest of my life being seen through the prism of my past, permanently labelled 'ex-anorexic' and, in all honesty, I pity anyone who has gone through this but feels differently. The thought that they see their illness as the most interesting thing about them is extremely sad, and any publication that encourages them to think that way should be despised at least as much as any fashion editor who tells a model that she's too fat.

However, I find it easier to talk about anorexia than to say nothing when people claim that it is entirely to do with models, or, conversely, that the media are blameless. Both positions are ridiculous and perpetuate the problem.

Eating disorders, like any mental illness, do not come from an outside agency, like a germ causes flu, or caffeine causes sleeplessness. They are a means of expressing extreme unhappiness, and it happens that the medium used to express it is food and the body, just as other people use drugs, alcohol or cutting. To suggest that fashion models cause eating disorders is as demeaning as saying beer adverts cause alcoholism, or watching *Trainspotting* brings on a pesky bout of heroin addiction.

Eating disorders – anorexia, bulimia and compulsive eating which is anorexia in its inverse form but conveying the same message through the same medium – have existed for centuries. Many women who were venerated as saints are now thought to have been anorexic.* Religion has venerated self-denying women at least as much as *Vogue* does.

This proves that cultural factors obviously play a part, yet, as repulsive and objectionable as those cultural messages are, and as insulting as they are to all women whether they are ill or not, these messages might create an environment in which eating disorders can fester, and go undiscovered for longer than they should, but they do not cause them.

This is not to excuse the fashion and celebrity industries and the general obsession with women's body shape in western culture. And it is certainly not to excuse them the way the fashion industry in particular tries to absolve itself, harrumphing that obesity is a more pressing problem so why all the attention on anorexia?[2] This is about as ridiculous as saying that one should not bother talking about infertility problems when teenage pregnancies are such an issue. The fashion industry has a very serious – and unsurprising – problem with eating disorders among those who work in it and, on that subject, it needs to be taken very much to task, and sticking in the occasional token fat model or celebrity on the runway is not good enough. Hell, it's not even good. It's just another physical extreme and suggests that the fashion

---

* *Holy Anorexia*, Rudolph M. Bell, University of Chicago Press, 1985.

[2] 'I'd just been on a trip to Minnesota, where I can only kindly describe most of the people I saw as little houses. And I just felt like there's such an epidemic of obesity in the United States. And for some reason everyone focuses on anorexia', Anna Wintour, US *Vogue*, *60 Minutes*, 17 May 2009.

industry has the same perspective on female body shape as – funnily enough – those who suffer from eating disorders: you can only be skinny or fat. There is no (healthy) middle ground.

But to see a newspaper publishing a photo of a clearly underweight model beneath an angry headline about how dangerous such a sight is to other people is the very definition of shooting the messenger when that messenger clearly needs help.

Cultural obsession with thinness is not irrelevant. When I was in hospital the doctors and my parents would try to assure me that all my fears about fatness and food were the illness talking. Yet when I was finally discharged, I was amazed to find myself in a culture that seemed to disprove all their assurances. These images of 'super-slim celebs' had been irrelevant to me when I became ill, but, now that I was trying to recover, they fed into all my thoughts and, to my still sick mind, validated them.

I read articles in women's magazines that could have been written by me when I was in hospital. There was Elizabeth Hurley saying she would commit suicide were she as fat as Marilyn Monroe. There was one well-known fashion writer describing her horror when her thighs, for the first time, touched after having a baby. There was an article in a very well-known fashion magazine about the joy of chunky-heeled boots giving one's legs 'the appearance of a frail baby fawn, just learning how to walk'. I felt like the paranoid in a cheesy horror movie who realises that his worst fears are, in fact, real. There is something very wrong when society condones an attitude reminiscent of the beliefs I held when I was mentally ill. And for a while, I used this as an excuse not to get better. If models, actresses and other women didn't eat and obsessed about weight, then why should I have to change? These things didn't make me ill, but they did make it harder to recover.

The bizarre value attributed to women's bodies – whether it's a fashion magazine demanding skinniness of its models or a tabloid newspaper praising a footballer's wife's 'perfect curves' – can, to someone who is looking for a way to articulate their unhappiness, present, subconsciously, a perfect solution. When one finds it hard to vocalise one's true feelings, and when one's own body seems like the medium that speaks the loudest to outsiders anyway, a twisted logic follows. One's body suddenly looks like the most powerful tool to wield. But it's an unhappiness from within that makes one need to wield a tool in the first place.

Often friends and families of people suffering from eating disorders focus on the food. This is particularly common with anorexics when anxious outsiders just want to make the starving patient look less like a concentration camp prisoner and this is, certainly, the most pressing short-term issue, simply for their physical health. But it is not the cure. There are other issues, namely, why the patient got that way in the first place. Getting to one's target weight is by no means – as relatives of anorexics discover to their dismay – the cure.

It is the same thing with cultural factors. They play a part, and many more play a part than the media allow. But they are not the cause. Unfortunately, some things are too complex to be explained by lazy space-filling first-person journalism and too ugly to be illustrated with a photo of Kate Moss.

Every dating guide you'll ever need

Do you ever look at those girls who have all the guys chasing after them and wonder what it is that they know but you don't? And then do you laugh ruefully at your silly paranoia because you know such talk is crazy insecurity talk? Well, guess what? There really ARE tricks to getting guys and, yes, everyone knows them but you. It's just like that time you didn't realise South Africa was its own separate country as opposed to a descriptive term for the southern part of the continent, but far more important.

Perhaps you are thinking, But wait! Can 50 per cent of the human race REALLY be affected in EXACTLY the same way by a series of tricks? Are things like individual personalities and past histories actually irrelevant when it comes to emotional responses and it all comes down to gender? And is it really worth having a relationship if you have to 'trick' the other person into it, you know, like an evil witch in a fairy tale casting a spell over a cherubic victim, and would you respect them if they fell for it? The answers, in order, are yes, yes, yes and who cares – at least you're with someone.

You see, men and women really are different creatures and while I'm not sure they actually come from different planets (!!!), sweeping generalisations about the genders can definitely be made, such as that men are dumb and women are crazy; or men are cavemen and women are cavemakers; or men are burgers and women are cupcakes. Whatever, they're all true! Once you decide which generalisation has some vague connection to any of your past relationships and therefore sums up the entire human species, you're halfway to your happy ending. With the help of this little guide, you'll see that you won't have to change anything about yourself to get your man, other than your behaviour, personality, natural desires and looks. Once you do all that, you can have ANY man eating out of your hand. Yes, I said ANY man. The only stress you're going to have in your life now is … which guy to choose!

First of all, how to meet this special someone? You need to break out of your usual social circle as that pond is too small for you to fish in – aim for the ocean! Give internet dating a go – honestly, EVERYONE'S doing it these days (except anyone who ever advocates that you try it) and how about joining an evening class? Not a girly one like 'vegetarian cooking' or 'beginners French' because you'll only meet girls and gays there, which would be a total waste of your time and money. Be ruthless and choose ones that don't interest you at all but sound hot and hetero, like 'car maintenance' and 'how to make your own app'. But also bear in mind that when you meet someone that way there is a risk that you'll have nothing at all in common, especially if you met him in an evening class that doesn't interest you at all or on some internet site where decisions are based purely on aesthetics.

Now you've got someone in your sights – what next? Well, guys can be incredibly slow, so you pretty much have to hit him over the head with a stick to make him take the hint. A guy won't ask a girl out if he thinks there's a chance he might get rejected, so make it super obvious that you're into him: smile all the time, hang out where he hangs out (but not in a stalker way, natch!) and touch his arm as often as possible. That's code for 'I give amazing blow jobs', just as twirling your hair means 'My breasts are perfection' and touching your neck means 'I love threesomes!' Everyone knows that!

Also, remember that nothing turns a guy on more than a girl who is hard to get. They're programmed that way, it's biological – you know, the whole hunter-gatherer thing? Make him have to hunt you (in a non-rapist way, obvs). So be aloof, ignore him, pretend you don't even know his name – it will intrigue him. You know what they say about treating a guy mean – it keeps him (or in this case, makes him!) keen! This is – to paraphrase the title of this chapter's favourite book – Why Men Marry Bitches! As everyone knows, if the title of a dating manual says it, it must be true.

Now he's asking you out on a hot date. A lot of women make the simple mistake of expecting the guy to make all the arrangements. Guys HATE this! The truth is – and I hope this doesn't sound too creepy! – the ideal woman for most men is, and always will be, their mother. So take charge and make suggestions about where you guys should have your hot first date, such as that cool retro bowling alley you read about in a Sunday supplement magazine, or maybe a trip to the zoo, which is an adorably quirky suggestion. Being with a capable woman makes a man feel protected and he'll LOVE the sense that he's with a girl who knows about the latest hot things. No guy wants a helpless woman! Except those who do. Guys love to feel manly and don't want to feel mothered so let him take charge. When he asks what you want to do on a date, tell him whatever he wants to do. This is always the right answer in all contexts, from social to sexual. Any other answer will – guaranteed – make him think you're a bossy, high-maintenance shrew.

Similarly, there is a lot of confusion over whether on a first date the bill should be split or whether traditional is still best and the guy should pay. Easy. It should be both. No guy wants to be with a gold-digger so make it clear from the beginning that you are soooo not that by paying your share. He will, though, probably think you're a grandstanding feminist who is financially emasculating him. Seriously, your wallet is almost the least sexy accessory you can bring on a date, second only to a chastity belt!

It's his primal instinct to be the provider: thwart him in that goal and he will lope back off to his cave like an injured animal and feast on carcasses, i.e. masturbate to internet porn.

But we're getting ahead of ourselves here. You haven't even had the date yet! A lot of women wonder, is there an outfit that is guaranteed to make a guy fall in love with me? Well, of course, all guys are different but all guys are also exactly the same so go for the look that works every time: an unbelievably hot dress, stacked heels, red lipstick, hair messed in a way that says high-maintenance nightmare but smoking hot sex that involves some kind of paraphernalia. Because, let's face it, we all know what guys want: Angelina Jolie. They want a girl who is a super-confident, demanding nightmare and will make their friends unbelievably jealous of all the athletic sex they are getting. Also, nothing looks sexier than a V-neck sweater, a tight pair of jeans, heels or pretty flats and natural hair. It's a look that suggests low-maintenance sweetness, with sex that is cosy as opposed to scary. Because, let's face it, we all know what guys really want: Jennifer Aniston – a girl who looks like a laugh and a great future wife. Well, all guys except Brad Pitt, of course.

The menu arrives – what to order? Obviously, you have to stay slim but you need to give the impression that you are effortlessly slim. Making an effort reveals that you are, in a way, cheating and if you reveal you have to work to stay thin he'll instantly think – no doubt correctly – that after you snare him you'll stop making an effort for him and you'll relax into your normal state of fatness. Also, needing to make an effort just isn't, you know, cool. Anyway, no guy wants to be with a woman who worries about calories – it's just boring, which is almost as bad as being fat. Remember *When Harry Met Sally*? And remember how long it took Harry to propose to Sally after he saw how fussy she was when she ordered food in the restaurant? All that 'on the side' business? Well, unless you have thirteen years to spare before you get that ring on your finger, don't ask to swap those fries for a salad – just starve yourself for the whole of the next day to make it up! Take a tip from all those glamorous actresses and models: have you ever noticed how, whenever they give interviews to glossy magazines over lunch, they always order something improbably calorific that the journalist can then voyeuristically coo about in her piece? This is to prove to readers not only how 'normal' the thin and beautiful actress or model is, but, conversely, how 'effortlessly slim' they are, which would seem to disprove the normalcy, but no matter. Whereas some people save their caloric binges for special occasions like birthdays, Christmas or, in your case, dates, models and actresses save theirs for interviews with fashion magazines, and then starve themselves the rest of the time. This is one of the few examples of *Vogue* encouraging someone to order a giant plate of carbs, but such is the importance of the illusion of 'effortless' slimness, and it will be just as effective on your guy as it is on a celebrity's fans.

Admittedly, one thing you need to bear in mind is – shhh, this is the great secret about guys that no one ever talks about! – that guys actually PREFER girls to have a little meat on them. It's true! They love your curves and think they're sexy. This is why the models in magazines for men are so much curvier than they are in magazines for women: women value skinniness, men don't. They like something to hold on to. Although men do like women to be petite and delicate and make them feel like a big strong man so when I say, 'men like curves', what I really mean, of course, is that men like a size 8 girl with double D boobs. So make sure that's how your weight gets distributed.

Regarding how much alcohol you should drink, you just need to find that precise amount that is enough for him to think you are drunk enough to make a move on, but not so much that he assumes you're an alcoholic STD-ridden slattern who he'll never call again after he nails you tonight. It is a very precise amount, as elusive as the *Daily Mail*'s ideal weight for a woman before it starts accusing her of being either disgustingly obese or enviably anorexic.

Some of you are still not sure how you should behave in the sack. Really, did our sisters win the sexual revolution for nothing?! Look, here's the sitch: as with drinking and *Daily Mail* weight, you need to find that sweet spot (so to speak!!!) wherein he's totally wowed by your sexual skills, but not so wowed that he'll assume you're a total whore. So you need to be good (and VERY comfortable wearing mesh anal dental floss for underwear on those special occasions!), but not too good. I don't know, maybe scrape him with your teeth occasionally. You know what I'm talking about.

Now you've slept with him and he promised to call – but forty-nine hours have passed and you haven't heard anything. What to do? Well, the answer is, nothing. Sure, feminism's success has allowed you to sleep with him without then having to sport a scarlet letter, but you're still not allowed to call him the morning(s) after. If a guy calls a girl the day after, he looks like a gentleman, if a girl calls a guy she looks like a sad crazy stalker. Feminism is all very good for things like, you know, better pay but when it comes to romance, you can't force progress on primal instinct. Sorry, but you're as stuck as Anne Elliot in *Persuasion* after Captain Wentworth leaves, paralysed by the social mores of the day into near spinsterhood, even though the social mores specifically dictate that all women should be coupled up and married asap.

(Incidentally, you should during all this time torture yourself by imagining that he DID send you a text only it went missing. You know, like in *Jean de Florette* in which Florette's letter telling her lover that they have a son goes missing and because of that, both she and he have lonely lives of misery, she turns their son into a hunchback, the father unwittingly later kills him and Gérard Depardieu ends up having to hump around that pillow up the back of his peasant shirt for that whole film. THAT'S TOTALLY WHAT'S GOING TO HAPPEN TO YOU. So for the sake of your future son and for actors everywhere, maybe you should call him. Except obviously if you do you are a crazy woman and you will end up alone and better to be a mother of a hunchback than a crazy spinster, right?)

Similarly, despite being a woman, Mother Nature is really not on our side when it comes to relationships and timing: you need to bank that man, any man, pronto. If that means you get divorced later because you panicked in your late twenties and married someone who got on your nerves by the second date, well, at least you can say you were married, right? Better divorced with two kids at forty than single at thirty-five!

So, as unromantic as it sounds, ladies, you really have to get him to seal the deal as quickly as possible. To do this, never let yourself forget, not for one single moment, that WITH EVERY SECOND YOU ARE BECOMING LESS AND LESS FERTILE AND THERE ARE MORE AND MORE HOT TWENTY-SOMETHINGS EMERGING INTO THE MARKETPLACE BEHIND YOU WHO ARE PUSHING YOU FURTHER OUT OF THE COMPETITION AND IF YOU HAVEN'T LOCKED A GUY DOWN BY THIRTY AND HAD A BABY BY THIRTY-TWO YOU WILL, AT BEST, END UP MARRIED TO THE GUY IN ACCOUNTS WITH HALITOSIS AND HAVE A BABY WITH A HAND FOR A HEAD AND EVERYONE WILL KNOW IT IS ALL YOUR FAULT FOR HAVING BEEN SO SELFISHLY SINGLE FOR SO LONG OR, AT WORST, YOU'LL BE ALONE, UNLOVED AND FORGOTTEN ABOUT IN YOUR HAGGISH STATE AND CAST OUT OF SOCIETY. IS THAT A NEW HAIR ON YOUR CHIN? IS THAT A GREY HAIR? A DROOPING BOOB? A DROPPING BUTTOCK? A DISAPPEARING JAWLINE? LOOK AT YOU, YOU'RE TURNING INTO A CRONE. WHO WILL WANT YOU BY THIS TIME NEXT YEAR? YOU NEED TO TRICK A GUY NOW INTO MARRYING YOU BEFORE YOUR INNER MISS HAVISHAM FULLY EMERGES. YOU NEED TO GET

MARRIED NOW YOU NEED TO GET MARRIED NOW
YOU NEED TO GET MARRIED NOW OR YOU WILL
NEVER HAVE SEX AGAIN MARRIED NOW MARRIED
NOW MARRIED NOW MARRIED NOW NOW NOW.

But also, never let him know that you are thinking this.
Even though you are bombarded with this message from
pretty much every form of media every day all day, if you are
weak enough to let the man in your life know that you have
been affected by it he will think that you are desperate and
after his vibrant sperm, and even though that's how you've
been taught to see yourself and men, that must not be how
you let YOUR man see you as he will be out the door faster
than you can say 'vaginal herpes'. Just as you need to
maintain the not-at-all-creepy illusion that you are as
hairless as a child but also his sexual plaything, you need to
pretend that even though you live in a world that is obsessed
with women's fertility and marital choices, you don't have
any insecurities at all about those issues. In fact, you are
totally blasé about the whole thing! You're just having fun
together, right? But yeah, you do need to get married now.

(Oh, and while we're on the subject of hairlessness, some
of you might wonder whether buying into the porn aesthetic
compromises their feminist credentials. The answer, of
course, is yes it does, but not doing so compromises the risk
of not having sex. Many have queried nineteenth-century art
critic John Ruskin's take on various artists but on one subject
he proved remarkably prescient: women's pubic hair. Ruskin's
knowledge of the feminine form began and ended with
Greek to Victorian sculpture and so, on his wedding night, he
was allegedly so horrified by his foolishly unwaxed wife's full
bush that he never consummated his marriage. This tale is
often reiterated as a slur on Ruskin but the poor guy's only

mistake was being born 150 years too early. Ladies, learn from Mrs Ruskin's mistake and make it your pre-date ritual to torture every single hair on your body, either by straightening it, tweezing it, plucking it, waxing it or lasering it, and, ideally, if you really want to make sure you get laid, all five. One could – if one had the time – marvel at the strange correlation between the rise in popularity of extensions and growing obsession with Rapunzel-like locks on top of a woman's head, and the expectation of hairlessness from below her neck, suggesting that women could save themselves a lot of money if they simply did tonsorial crop rotation on their body and glued the depilatoried pubic hair on to their scalp. But I'm afraid, actually, one doesn't have time, what with fitting in an eyebrow threading appointment, a highlights touch-up and a blow dry before lunchtime.)

Which brings me to the next point: what if you've been with your guy for more than a year but he still hasn't got down on that bended knee? Well, some guys just need a little push and a judicious fake pregnancy, or even a real one, because you 'forgot' to take the Pill one morning ('I guess the coil didn't work' – sometimes you gotta be grateful for how DUMB guys are about contraception!) is often the wake-up call he needs. No guy can choose for himself when he's ready to give up his Xbox and drinking sessions with his mates, so he'll secretly be relieved to have the choice made for him. Remember, though, that no guy likes to feel railroaded into a decision, let alone lied to, so there is a very good chance that your plan will completely backfire and he'll either leave you or resent you for ever. You cannot nag a guy into marriage. You cannot nag him into anything. All guys are really just little boys in manly bodies and it is their natural instinct to rebel against a maternal figure. So never express any of your own wishes at all, or at least not overtly. You can either spend your life subtly manipulating him which will make you swiftly lose all respect for him because he cannot see your ham-fisted puppet-master techniques, or simply staying silent, stifling your own worries and desires, and waiting for him to come to a decision on his own.

Perhaps some of you are noticing that one particular word has not been mentioned in this chapter: love. Perhaps you are thinking that you'd always thought marriage was more than just something you were supposed to 'achieve', something you were supposed to do to prove your normality, like learning how to drive and feeling some kind of sentimentality for M&S. Perhaps you buck against this whole idea of a 'marriage market', with its intimations of valuation, false advertising and obligation and think that two people should come together if they love one another, not to stave off future loneliness and to prevent other people from baggsying them first. These are all very noble opinions and hopefully the warmth of them will keep you cosy over the next fifty years of lonely nights, you deluded spinster.

Finally, to quote William Shakespeare, this above all: to thine own self be true.

But, you know, not too much.

You don't need Winona Ryder to tell you how to live your life

Important people like talk show hosts and rent-a-shrinks who selflessly take time out of their busy practice to give random quotes to women's magazines and something called 'lifestyle TV programmes' are fond of rolling out various old saws about what shapes one's identity as an adult. All these saws can be summed up as 'it's your fault or it's someone else's fault'. In fancy terms, this is the nature versus nurture dichotomy.

However, there is another possible factor, one that is almost always overlooked and yet straddles both of the above schools of thought: the fictional character that you discovered as a child and became not just your guide to the world beyond your family, but the lens through which you for ever see yourself, even long after you've forgotten the original source material that truly shapes you. In other words, it's the character you over-identified with as a kid.

This is not to say that if your favourite character as a child was, let's say, Linus from *Peanuts* that you then spend the rest of your life dragging around a blanket, but you might see yourself as downtrodden and helplessly beleaguered by exterior malevolent forces, represented in this case, of course, by the glorious Lucy van Pelt. Similarly, if you were devoted to Anne of Green Gables, as good as your taste in literary characters obviously is, it might be time to stop thinking of yourself as the scrappy teenage outsider endearingly besotted with poetry, particularly if you are now thirty-three.

It is not the self-indulgence of such over-identification that is the problem here. Personally, I've always thought that self-indulgence gets a misguidedly bad rap, not least because smug self-denial always struck me as a lot more self-indulgent than, say, an occasional massage.

Rather, it's the limiting perspectives that these fictional self-images provide that is the problem: limiting, and often wrong.

A person's fictional self-image is an indication of how they saw themselves as a child, writ large. But taking it as a given that one's self-perception is about as accurate as the reflection one sees in a fairground mirror, then the view one had of oneself as a child is not only at least a little skewed but (hopefully) very out of date by the time one reaches adulthood.

The fact that these images come from the fictional world is relevant, too, as fiction, particularly children's fiction, generally concludes with a happy ending. Thus, the fictional self-images represent the hope, even assumption of a future happy ending, while also appearing to present a handy template of how one should behave in order to achieve it. Ironically, though, their inherently limiting nature might actually achieve precisely the opposite.

For example, I shall tell you a story from a journal far more reliable than any psychology magazine or study commissioned to back up some doubtful claim a commercial company wishes to make in its advertising campaign. It comes from the journal of me.

It was the evening of 11 March 2010, the day after – as I'm sure I hardly need to inform all of you – former eighties teen idol Corey Haim had died. Naturally, my immediate response to the news of Haim's death had been to arrange a modern-day celebrity wake, which is when one immerses oneself in the early work of a recently deceased, usually self-destructive, possibly long-forgotten and probably long-derided celebrity and proceeds to insist that they were the greatest artist ever born and, honestly, you always knew they were under-appreciated, even if you hadn't actually thought about them for at least a decade.

As is the way with the ritual nature of the modern-day celebrity wake, I limited myself to the high points of Haim's career and adopted convenient amnesia towards the likes of *Dream a Little Dream*, to say nothing of *The Two Coreys*, the deeply upsetting reality TV programme Haim starred in the year before his death, a show that proved, one, that Haim's ravaged body had become its own metaphor for the cost his youthful fame exacted on his soul and, two, that reality TV producers must take Bikram yoga to achieve the spinal flexibility necessary to stoop down towards the depths they so eagerly seek.

And so, I worked my way through *The Lost Boys* and I worked my way through *Murphy's Romance*. Dusk was soon closing in, cloaking my ritual in the respectful shroud of a purpled sky, just as I reached for the film that especially intrigued me – *Lucas*, one of Haim's earliest films which he made when he was fourteen and which I vaguely remembered loving as a child, but all specifics were foggy. The specifics turned out to be wonderful, if utterly heartbreaking, not just because of the film's gently moving plot which bears more than a few similarities to *Rushmore*, made fourteen years later, but because of the proof it gave that Haim really had once been an extraordinarily talented actor. Roger Ebert said in his review of this film with retrospectively shattering irony, 'He creates one of the most three-dimensional, complicated, interesting characters of any age in any recent movie. If he can continue to act this well, he will never become a half-forgotten child star, but will continue to grow into an important actor. He is that good.'

Lucas is the delicate story of the eponymous skinny, nerdy little boy (Corey Haim) who falls in love with a new girl at his school (Kerri Green). She, however, likes the hot jock (Charlie Sheen) so, in an attempt to win his lady love round, Lucas joins the football team and achieves little in the way of sporting glory but a great deal in the way of physical injuries. He is humiliated and heartbroken, so much so that he doesn't notice that his similarly awkward and somewhat boyish friend (Winona Ryder) clearly has a crush on him. Ryder – one of the most beautiful women ever born – plays an allegedly plain girl, one relegated to the sidelines of the movie and reduced to saying things like, 'Not everybody gets to be pretty, you know.' (It is a strange quirk of eighties movies that the actresses who play the kooky high school outsiders are invariably more gorgeous than those cast as the allegedly pretty prom queens, as proven by the early careers of Ryder, Ally Sheedy and the original *Teen Wolf* film. In fact, their 'kookiness' seems to lie solely in the shade of their hair – brunette – whereas the prom queens are always, ALWAYS, blonde, proving that the Hitchcockian dichotomy of women's hair colour reflecting their desirability did not die with Grace Kelly. That I myself am a brunette has in no way influenced my sense of injustice at this trope.)

Now, the first thing to say is that if a Corey Haim film had to shape my entire life, I am very glad it was not *License to Drive*. The second thing is this film is perhaps as good as Lindsay Lohan's career to serve as evidence for the prosecution against allowing children to appear in movies when one considers how the then fresh-faced leads, Haim, Sheen and Ryder, ended up. The third thing to note is that Jeremy Piven has apparently been playing the same part – the bullying asshole – for twenty-five years, from *Lucas* to *Say Anything* to, of course, *Entourage*, which is, I guess, um, a compliment? Well done on embodying assholism so brilliantly, Jeremy!

And the last thing to say about *Lucas* is that halfway through watching it I finally realised what my fictional self-identity was: it was a secondary, maybe even tertiary character from an almost wholly unknown Corey Haim movie. Did I mention I have a degree in English literature?

Pretty much from the ages of eight to thirty-two, I saw myself as the character type Ryder plays in *Lucas*: the slightly weird and often overlooked brunette, always on the outside, never getting to experience the main plot lines, simmering away in a constant stew of unrequited crushes. Ryder's influence on me outlasted her own career by about a decade. A conviction for shoplifting is no bar to her having a role in my life. I am a lot less picky than Hollywood, in many respects.

While this film probably didn't change my life as much as it did that of the poor three kids who starred in it, it did definitely leave a subconscious imprint. Maybe if I hadn't watched this film sarcasm and world-weary asides would not have been my default teenage reactions to all comments made to me by the opposite sex, because I didn't want them to think that they could possibly be talking seriously to me, or that I cared if they didn't. And maybe I would not have favoured clothes that looked like they came from not just Kensington Market but the remainders racks in Kensington Market (which, in fact, they did) in the belief that to dress otherwise might have made people think that I was – hilariously – trying to dress prettily, when I was not the pretty girl, I was the platonic girl, and such an obvious sartorial show that I did not know my place would have rendered me laughable, which is, of course, every teenager's greatest fear.

If this were an eighties film, my epiphany would have been accompanied also by the similar realisation that the reason I couldn't even give it away in my teenage years was because I subconsciously chose to develop crushes on boys who would never like me back because that fitted in with my idea of myself as an always-the-friend-never-the-girfriend kinda gal, and being that kind of girl made me special, superior, sensitive, even, and it also meant that I would, eventually, get the boy of my dreams – because that's what happens in the movies, right? Maybe, too, I would also have looked back and, in the retrospective creases of my mind, realised that the quiet geeky boy I was always friends with at school actually loved me – and he was great! And still single! Strike up the eighties power ballad! Roll credits!

But I do not live in an eighties film and my geeky male school friend is not only unlikely to have harboured any secret lust for me but he is also not single, as he has been living with a gentleman by the name of Jeremy for the past five years. It is entirely likely that the reason I led a teenage life more prim than that of a nineteenth-century Quaker owes more to the fact I dressed like the Grim Reaper in long black skirts and deeply unfortunate oversized tops that managed to be both goth and tie-dye, two genres that should never be mixed, as opposed to any cleverness on the part of my subconscious.

But that is not the point. The point is, if I'd known all this years earlier, maybe I would have put some thought into how I actually wanted to dress, look and behave because I would have understood that I didn't need to be constrained to playing the part of the platonic, misunderstood friend. Unlike Ryder, I wasn't actually cast in that part by anyone, other than myself.

True, letting go of one's fictional self-image does also mean letting go of the idea that life is somehow like a book or movie and that a happy ending is, one day, guaranteed, a relinquishment that is the grown-up version of learning who Santa Claus really is. But just as that festive childhood trauma comes with the silver lining of understanding how much your parents love you, giving up the idea that life is like a film or book also has an upside. It is only then that you can appreciate how much freedom you have in regard to how you live your life and if you want to be that kind of girl who does, occasionally, wear something other than a long raggedy black skirt and matching top, you truly, truly can. And you don't need to wait for Corey Haim to die to do this.

But do you like him?

Not very long ago I discovered a website that – I don't think it's hyperbolic to say – sums up everything about love and the female species. Like many things on the internet, this website captures the dark and tragically unexaggerated truth of the human soul and, in doing so, disproves not just the idea that we are in a post-feminist world, but makes one question Darwinism.

This website, HeTexted.com, is brilliant in its simplicity and devastating in its emotional truth. How it works is this: women – generally young, generally American – engage in text conversations with a guy, often one they have previously 'hooked up with', as young American women tend to put it these days, apparently. The texts from the guy baffle the women to such an extent that they send them in to HeTexted. com where they are posted in full, and strangers vote on whether the texts suggest the young man is 'into you' or 'not into you.' That's it.

Hours, no, *days* of my life have since been lost to this quicksand of a website. Each text conversation provides, not just a glimpse into how Romeo and Juliet would have read if emoticons and acronyms had existed in the sixteenth century ('I like you and not just for sex lol ;)'), but a gawp at the futility of progress. And partly what makes it all so mindblowingly terrifying is that it is the high tech version of reality. A bunch of female friends all huddled together, parsing another friend's mobile, reading the tea leaves of some blithe suitor's casual text: this is such a common image of female bonding that it is as clichéd as a shopping trip, yet remains no less true for it.

HeTexted.com captures the determined triumph of optimism over the obvious ('He texted "I don't want you to get too attached" – does he like me?'), the insistence on finding meaning where there is none ('I sent him a text, he texted back "Thanks" – what does that mean?') and the twanging thrum of insecurity when security is offered ('He texted "I love u" – is he just not that into me any more?'), all wrapped in the constant doubt in one's own judgement. Each posted text is an anguished plea: 'Say he likes me! Make him like me! Oh God, please confirm to me that he likes me!'

But despite spending days (weeks) scrolling, hypnotised, through these HeTexted.com conversations, each followed by frantic online discussions of the possible feelings men felt towards the women, I did not encounter a single instance of the woman mentioning her feeling about the man.

Generalisations are all abhorrent and gender generalisations are among the worst of all. But in all my years of being a woman and spending time primarily with women I have noticed an intriguing trait that seems specifically, if by no means universally or even exclusively, popular among my gender: a reluctance to consider what they themselves actually want. A common example of this is when a woman, instead of saying what she would like to do, tries to anticipate what the other person in the conversation wants to do. For this woman, a friendly chat is less an exchange of ideas than an exhausting and often rather frantic attempt to read what the other person would like her to say, which opinion she ought to express in order to be liked or even just keep the conversational peace. It is easy to spot such a species by her anxious smile and frequent howl of 'Oh, whatever you want!' These women need to write in lipstick across their bathroom mirror, 'No – what do *I* want?', and repeat it to themselves ten times every morning and again before bed, while brushing their teeth and washing their face.

Women – through films, through books, through pop culture, through society, maybe even through their own older female relatives – are still, 50 years after *The Feminine Mystique*, taught that their role in life is to be nice. To be sweet. To keep things smooth. To be the girlfriend in the movie who exists only in relation to the male protagonist. And most of all, to be liked – to please people.

None of this is new, of course, which is precisely what makes it so infuriating. Still, today, women who speak up – whether as politicians, activists, writers or celebrities – are, at best, seen by the press as intriguing specimens, held up and inspected like a new species of lizard, or, more commonly, dismissed as mouthy, batty harridans. And if this woman dares to be childless and single, well, that only proves her unnaturalness and comedy potential.

No matter how many alleged girl power and riot grrrl phases pop culture goes through, women are ultimately taught that, sure, making a fuss and claiming independence is all very well, but ultimately it's in the pursuit of appealing to a man and playing the expected, conventional female role.* Sure, you can shout and stomp about as a female pop singer and sing about being an independent woman*² or a monster,*³ but you'd better look sexy doing it. And if you can't do that, then you'd better at least make your serious point in a funny and/or girlish voice, and with a smiley emoticon at the end of the sentence: 'See! No need to fear me! Just kidding!!!! Whatever you want!!!!!!'

Many women internalise all manner of lessons from such messages and one lesson that HeTexted.com brings to light is that a woman should not think of her own needs, nor form her own opinions. She should kowtow to someone else's desires and follow someone else's cues, and nowhere is this more obvious than in her interaction with the opposite sex.

Three things are going on in such interactions: an instinct for people-pleasing, a disregard for her own desires and an overestimation of the importance of male validation. Until embarrassingly late in life, it rarely occurred to me to ask myself whether I liked the chap in front of me who appeared to be asking me on a date – I was simply flattered and relieved to be asked, and became obsessed with him accordingly. I didn't want to sleep with these people (after all,

---

* The anthem of this mentality is, of course, Beyoncé's 'Single Ladies', an allegedly defiant anthem about female independence in which an ex-boyfriend's regret at not having married the singer of the anthem is seen as some great triumph. Beyoncé's 'Girls Run the World' is equally irritating in a similar way, with its suggestion that while females are strong and independent, they are – rest assured! – still just 'girls'. And, incidentally, for the record, neither girls nor women are anywhere close to 'running the world'.

*2 Beyoncé, again. For the record, I do like Beyoncé. Just not all the time.

*3 Lady Gaga who, for the record, I don't care about one way or another.

I didn't even fancy them, which perhaps explains how I managed to keep my virginity for so long it practically became illegal): I just wanted them to admire me and to keep admiring me. To validate me.

Maybe if I hadn't been such a shy mouse and had opened myself up to more approaches I wouldn't have placed so much value on the few I got and would have learned earlier to ask myself what I actually wanted from a suitor. As it was, though, I spent approximately two-thirds of my waking hours between the ages of fourteen to thirty myopically obsessing and pining over men whom I didn't even like. Sometimes I like to depress myself by pondering what else I could have accomplished in all that wasted time. Cured cancer, perhaps. Learned plumbing skills. Cleaned out my closet (although let's not go crazy here).

Clearly, this craven reaction to any signs of male appreciation is not a universal tendency among my sex – if it was, a whole genre of high school movies wouldn't even exist – and the admiration I feel for sixteen-year-old girls who possess enough confidence and self-awareness to know they don't need to please all men is akin to the kind I feel for people who grow up speaking more than one language. Ah, to possess such skills from the start! To have a mind so different to my own! But for others, it's a mentality that becomes hard to shake and often misinterpreted by others as sluttishness and shameful neediness. Maybe it is in some but for most, I would wager, it is merely the internalisation of messages that women are still constantly fed: appeal to all, especially to men, and male validation is the only validation that really matters.

To attract a man, the message goes, proves that you, as a woman, have some kind of worth, that you are a proper woman, as an unattractive woman is barely a woman at all. This explains the sense of triumph that comes with it: 'Hurrah! I won the man race! I'm saved! A man likes me – he really, really likes me!' (This bit should be internally shrieked in a Sally-Field-at-the-Oscars voice.) Hence the tone of blind panic at the thought of that validating appreciation being taken away, a panic that is so all-consuming that the young woman does not have the mental space to consider if she ever even liked the man: 'Wait! Come back! Without you, I'm nothing! Even though you're kind of mean to me, we have nothing in common and I need my friends to decipher your text messages to find any crumb of loving in them – please, please come back!'

It's not a part of oneself that brings much pride: it's one that has proven resistant to feminism, even in the most proudly feminist of souls, and that is at least partly because it reflects a social attitude towards women that has proven similarly reluctant to move forward.

But as the feminist movement in general has proven for over a century now, just because society is resistant to change doesn't mean that women must be, too. I'm a big fan of the Bechdel Test, which I've mentioned elsewhere in this book, which tests whether a film has a gender bias. So, with all respect to Alison Bechdel, I would like to coin the Hadley Test for all women who find themselves in a similar situation to those poor souls who turn to HeTexted.com or, more commonly, to their beleaguered friends for help in understanding not what he is trying to say to you, but what you should say to yourself:

1. Do you actually like this guy as a person or just as the concept of a generic boyfriend?

2. Does he make you feel happy in yourself or are you slightly hysterical with insecurity? (And if the latter, do you know that's a bad thing and life doesn't have to be that way?)

3. Do you like him so much that it doesn't matter to you that you need your friends to translate his messages for you?

4. When you are asked 'What do you want,' is your first instinct to think 'What does he want'?

5. No. What do YOU want?

You're never too old for Topshop

Nothing – not meth, not sunbeds, not even the passage of time – is more ageing than you saying you're too old for something. This is not because other people will then look at you anew and see you as old,* but because it is a deeply depressing thing to say, and you will depress no one more than yourself. Even Richard Ashcroft – not a man known for shunning the mopey side of life – found that 'all this talk of getting old/It's getting me down my love.' And quite right, too, because it is an utterly hopeless conversational cul-de-sac. When people worry about being 'too old', this is either a euphemism for 'too boring' or code for 'I thought I'd have done more with my life by now.' But ironically, the complaint only proves the former and exacerbates the latter. You probably could have cured cancer in all the time you spent talking about how old you are.

Music festivals, staying out late, trips to Topshop: the only factors preventing you from partaking of any of the above are

---

* The second most ageing thing is worrying what other people think of you. So frankly, fuck that shit.

stamina, free time and – for all the parents out there – access to babysitters. The age issue is merely a common background issue to all those factors; it is not the actual problem in and of itself. To waste time while you are doing any of the above worrying about how all the youngsters there will be laughing at you for trying to join in, Grandma, is akin to wondering what you were like in a past life – it is not just daft, it is irrelevant to the present time. As you might remember from when you yourself were a mere pupa, young people's eyesight is not fully formed and so they cannot actually see anyone who is older than themselves. This affliction, in fact, never goes away for most people. So while the thought that young people are as blind to you as you are, cruelly, to the pensioners you overtake in the street might jar somewhat, take consolation that it means they simply do not see you, do not care about you and, therefore, do not judge you. Revel in that and throw your arms in the air because you really, really shouldn't care.

Life is not like cinema classifications in which certain activities are *verboten* to those over a certain age. So while you might see many odd things in Topshop – boiler suits, underwear emblazoned, for no obvious reason, with images of Hello Kitty – one thing you won't see are mic'd-up heavies positioned around the room, ready to sidle up quietly behind any women over forty they spot flicking through the rah-rah skirt rails, pick her up by her elbows and carry her to the exit whispering quietly in her ear, 'Come along, madam, let's go to Phase Eight, shall we?'

You know your life has progressed when going to Glastonbury no longer conjures up an image of extraordinary hedonism but rather one of expensive babysitters, physical discomfort and driving nightmares and, really, you'd much rather stay home and watch the highlights on BBC4 over a bottle of Chablis. That is when you know you have outgrown Glastonbury. Worrying that you will look like an out-of-place oldster at the event might prove that you are too self-centred for fun (repeat: no one is looking at you), but not that you are too old for it.

In a world in which wrinkles are seen as something to airbrush and fill with weird chemicals, as opposed to being glorious badges of honour of a life well lived and full of laughter, clearly attitudes to age are upside down. This is proven by the aforementioned code of 'I'm too old' standing for 'I'm too boring.' What it should – and, secretly, even if the speaker doesn't know it, does – actually stand for is 'I'm too wise.' This does not mean 'wise' in the boring, snarky sense of the word, as in 'I used to like reading Jilly Cooper but now I prefer more intelligent literature, like Julian Barnes,' a classic example of the word 'intelligent' meaning the inverse of what the speaker thinks it does.

Rather being 'too old' really means 'wise enough to know how to do it properly, having learned from the mistakes of my youth'. Young people might have the smooth hands of Italian marble statues but they do not have something you have which is so much more important: years and years of embarrassing fuck-ups in their past from which to take heed. They still have to wander through the thorny forest whereas you're already in the enchanted Land of Experience (if not Infallibility).

Thus, it's not that you're 'too old' for Topshop; rather that you're wise enough to know that you should walk straight past the boiler suits and silly logoed underwear and head to the lovely smarter clothes – the longer dresses, the cropped trousers, the coats – that are hidden among the party dresses and skirts which are very popular but render the entire world your gynaecologist.

Topshop may be ostensibly intended for younger customers, and certainly its emphasis on clothes that would allow a passing stranger to give you a smear test without too much difficulty would suggest as such. But a store, and in particular its owner Philip Green, does not become such a behemoth without knowing what's what and what's what is that while younger customers will buy stupid things, older ones will buy more expensive ones because they have the money and, thus, the store will always, albeit discreetly, provide accordingly. Yes, it's ridiculous that fashion stores, high street and designer, think that putting the young clothes in the window will make them look trendier and more desirable, but smart retailers will provide for those born before 1992 somewhere in their vicinity.

Similarly, it's not that you're 'too old' for music festivals but rather that you're too smart to do them the way you used to, i.e. staying up for three days straight, pausing only occasionally to change your hotpants in the tent that you put up, somewhere, in the middle of some field, just behind that tree – oh no, not that one, maybe in the next field, oh fuck, some tree, fuck. Now, you know that camping is something only soldiers do, and generally not by choice, so you stay in a camper van or a nice little B & B nearby, and have an even better time than you did as a teenager because you have access to better plumbing and better intoxicants than the cheap booze you used to buy at the train station. You have the wisdom and, significantly, the money young people do not, and the fact that music festivals are so prohibitively expensive for most young people these days proves that even the music industry appreciates this obvious truth.

This is an important factor to remember whenever something makes you feel depressed about being older than sixteen. Yes, yes, we all know about the centuries' long veneration of female youth. Yet seeing as this stemmed from a time when most people lived until about thirty and was based on women's fertility, and we now live in a time when people live arguably too long and women can reproduce well into their sixties with a combination of luck and a slightly dodgy doctor, the hysterical obsession with youth today does seem a little odd. Until one considers whether maybe the reason the skincare and plastic surgery industries in particular encourage such insecurity about ageing is because people who have aged a little over the years have money to throw about.

It's pointless to harangue teenagers to buy anything more expensive than Noxzema pads because they can't afford it. Grown-ups, though, are a far more lucrative market, and as forty-somethings generally have more money than twenty-somethings, the more middle-aged the better as they're more likely to be able to afford a £395 acid peel. In short, think of the ageist culture that is all too dominant as being like the heartless cad who targets rich fools and gulls them out of their money. Don't be gulled, not by an industry that is aimed at turning women into self-hating masochists. In my more idealising moments, I'm amazed we live in a world in which such tactics are even legal. Telling women that they should torture their skin so as to resemble a younger complexion because that's the only desirable look is exactly the same as companies that flog 'whitening creams' to women with Asian and black skin, insinuating that only Caucasian faces are attractive.

Depressingly, if predictably, fashion magazines and TV makeover shows aimed at women are particularly keen on this kind of gulling. Fashion magazines do love themselves an easy double-page spread impudently telling women how to dress in each decade of their lives, advice that can generally be summed up as Longer, Duller, Beiger and More Expensive as Time Goes By. There will be sentences of the 'as you get older, good tailoring is key' variety, adding further proof to the generally held suspicion that fashion magazines are not written by humans but robots.

Then there are the TV makeover shows that became so popular in the past decade – and really, how could they not? Cheap and based entirely on making women get undressed and then humiliating them: it's just a wonder it took TV so long to hit upon this genius formula. The entire modus operandi of these shows is to make women feel that if their bodies show any sign of humanity, then they should exchange their happy colourful clothes for beige trousers and a tailored blazer. After all, good tailoring is key.

All this ageist nonsense plays into the idea that getting older is to stare down the barrel of boredom and beige trousers and therefore to have fun would render you laughable, a mere pink T-shirt away from being humiliated on national TV while a bossy presenter squeezes your boobs in front of a three-way mirror and explains precisely where you're going wrong in every aspect of your life. It is the sartorial and televisual equivalent of pushing older folk out on an ice float.

This is all utter and absolute cobblers. You are just as entitled to fun as you are to that one gorgeous dress that is lurking just in the corner in Topshop, past the playsuits and bandage miniskirts.

Getting older does not mean that fun times and fun fashion are out of reach to you: rather, that you know how to do fun properly, that you can afford better fun and, most and best of all, that you will never, ever be tempted to camp or buy any Hello Kitty underwear. Make use of your hard-won wisdom: dismiss the gulling fools. And darling, you're fabulous.

The ten commandments of being an unannoying vegetarian

WRITTEN BY A LIFELONG VEGETARIAN

1. Don't define yourself by what you do or don't eat. Being a vegetarian is a culinary choice, it is not a personality.
2. Please don't talk about your poo. Yeah, it's so much looser than when you were a carnivore, it's so much floatier and you're so much more regular: NOBODY WANTS TO KNOW. Please. Stop talking about your poo.
3. Don't preach. Too many vegetarians compensate for their reduced intake of protein by increasing their emissions of smugness. Yes, you love being a vegetarian; yes, it may be healthier than eating three portions of red meat a day (although not much if your diet now consists solely of buttered toast and spaghetti with parmesan). But to become a pushy vegetarian is the culinary equivalent of becoming a fanatical atheist: inherently contradictory and self-defeating. The ethos of vegetarianism is non-harming of animals and humans are animals and you are harming them with your annoying smugness and smug descriptions of your diet such as 'clean', 'light' and

'really, the way we're meant to eat'. So if this is your attempt to save more animals by converting others to your cause, it is guaranteed to backfire. Coating something in the sweaty sheen of self-righteousness never makes it more appetising. In fact, it is more likely to drive them straight to a bucket of *foie gras* as they seek to prove to themselves that they will never, ever be like you. So for the sake of the animals, have a hot cup of shut up.

4. Don't talk about your weight loss. Have you lost much weight since becoming a vegetarian? Have you? Have you really? Are your jeans so much looser? Do you just feel so much lighter? Really? Do you? You know what? No one cares.

5. Don't make your non-vegetarian friends eat in vegetarian restaurants. This is simply rude. Unless your friends want to eat in an abattoir, there is always something vegetarian on a restaurant menu. OK, there might not be much but there is something. There is not, however, any meat on the menu of a vegetarian restaurant and while you made the choice to give up meat and therefore limit your food options, your meat-eating companions did not. Furthermore, vegetarian restaurants, with their fake food on the menu, their over-earnest waiting staff and the general smell of smugness emanating from the kitchen, are unlikely to persuade your carnivorous friends that vegetarianism is anything other than for the condescending birds.

6. Do not eat Tofurkey, 'chick'n', or any other mock meat products. Eating synthetic meat products is a little like being married but still going to lap dancing clubs: if you're really so unhappy in your current arrangement, then you need to rethink your lifestyle because at the

moment you're just tormenting yourself with a deeply unsatisfying and, to be honest, pretty disgusting alternative. Moreover, it will just look to outsiders like being vegetarian means missing meat and having to make do with rehydrated protein products sculpted into the vague shape of drumsticks. Just get yourself some tofu, grill it, marinate it and eat it and don't pretend to yourself that it came from a farmyard.

7. Prepare your responses. As a vegetarian, you are going to face questions – quite possibly on a daily basis – from wags who think it's hilarious to harangue you about your dietary choices. You are likely to encounter the fascinating phenomenon of people who think this is an excellent manner of seduction on a first or second date, despite, one hopes, the scarcity of vegetarians who have ever been wooed into bed by someone pointing out the hypocrisy of wearing leather but scorning beef. So consider how you will deal with such verbal gadflies now so as not to be flustered at the time. Humour is the most effective manner of deflection, not least because it tends to shut the conversation down quick-smart rather than provoking a forty-five-minute debate about farming methods, which is rarely a passion starter. Here are some suggested answers to get you going:

★ **What about leather?**
I've just never liked the taste.

★ **Why are you a vegetarian?**
Because my mother's a cow.

✱ You know Hitler was a vegetarian

Yes, but so far I have resisted the urge to cause mass genocide. It's all about balance.

8. Help the animals. After all, that is pretty much the point of vegetarianism, right? So for every time you refrain from haranguing someone about their carnivorous ways, donate some money to animal charities. True, the former method is more fun, and cheaper, but no one ever said being a good vegetarian was easy.

9. Remember, the world is not your personal caterer. This means there will not always be vegetarian options, and that's not outrageous – surprising, sometimes, but not outrageous. So if a bunch of you meet at a restaurant where there isn't an acceptable vegetarian main course on the menu, don't insist that everyone ups sticks and finds somewhere else that suits your stomach: simply make do with a couple of side dishes and eat more when you get home. It's not that your needs are unimportant, rather that they're not more important than everyone else's. (And anyway, the side dishes are often the best things on the menu.) Similarly, when someone invites you to their house for a dinner party, think carefully about telling them beforehand you're a vegetarian. Do you really want them to feel obligated to make a special meal just for you when they have to worry about feeding the rest of the group? If they ask if you're a vegetarian, then yes, fine, tell them, but if not, and you turn up and the only thing on the table is a terrine of chicken curry, make do with some cheese and crackers from the kitchen and the dessert. Causing a self-centred fuss does not help the cause.

10. Don't go to eastern Europe. Or only do so if you like cabbage and potatoes A LOT. Otherwise, you will spend your entire time there whingeing about how unbelievably hungry you are. Similarly, should you ever need to lose some weight, go to South America as there will be nothing for you to ingest there other than vodka. You get to see that big Jesus statue, have a legitimate excuse to be drunk for the whole of your holiday and you are likely to drop three jean sizes. Win win win!

The Forwardthinkoriums

A long time ago, in a galaxy far far away, there was a planet called Forwardthinkorium. The people on Forwardthinkorium thought about the future. A lot. In fact, the only topic of conversation was wondering what was about to happen, what would happen and what will happen. Their other distinguishing features included their claw-like hands and their indefatigable jaw muscles, which they never tired of exercising. They also had difficulty in reading other people's facial expressions and reactions. But because they only mixed with one another, this was not a problem. They simply lived in their talkative, future-focused blithe way, causing neither offence nor hurt to anyone else.

One day, a group of Forwardthinkorium scientists decided to conduct an experiment. They wanted to find out if by doing something extremely dramatic they would sate the constant obsession of their fellow Forwardthinkoriums to know what was happening and never enjoying the present or allowing anyone else to do so either. So they planned to fly to a new little planet called Earth, still fuzzy in its infancy.

Surely, they thought, this would be enough. After all, what could top travelling to a new planet? Maybe then everybody could start using the present tense instead of always employing the future.

This hope turned out to be optimistic. As soon as the scientists' spaceship had taken off, the Forwardthinkoriums back on the planet were asking one another, 'When will the spaceship land?' 'What will the scientists do when they get to Earth?' 'How long will they stay there?' 'What will their journey back be like?' 'How will they land?' and 'Hey, what's on TV later?' They did not wonder how the scientists were at that moment enjoying the journey – which they were, immensely, as they had mocked up the inside of the spaceship to look exactly like the room with the chocolate lake in the 1971 film of *Willy Wonka and the Chocolate Factory* (minus the tube in which Augustus Gloop gets stuck which at least one six-year-old found so terrifying she had to be carried out of the cinema by my mum, I mean, her mum). But to wonder such a question would be to focus on the present, which went against the Forwardthinkorium practice. Instead they busily asked one another questions about the future but these questions, as all Forwardthinkorium questions were, could only be rhetorical. After all, they were all only Forwardthinkoriums, they weren't psychics.

Fortunately, the scientists inside the spaceship could not hear all this chatter so it did not spoil their journey. But because they themselves had spent so much time talking about the future (lest we forget, the scientists were Forwardthinkoriums too), they forgot to make actual plans for the future and, thus, they neglected to bring enough petrol for the return journey.

It was not until they landed on Earth and had a little toddle about the place that they realised that they were stuck there.

But truth be told, the scientists did not mind this a jot. Earth was as interesting as they'd hoped, full of people who used the present tense, and enough Forwardthinkorium scientists had come on the trip so they needn't ever get homesick. So in short, everything worked out well for the Forwardthinkorium scientists. It's today's earthlings who suffer.

Without wishing on any level to sound planetist, it is occasionally difficult for species from different planets to coexist. Misunderstandings take place, unintended insults abound, irritations ensue. One sees this with especial clarity when a descendant from the Forwardthinkoriums mixes with an earthling. To a Forwardthinkorium, there is nothing wrong with barracking an earthling with endless questions about their future plans, such as when they will have a boyfriend or, if the earthling already has a boyfriend, when they will move in together, get married, spawn, spawn further.

But there have been tales of earthlings who have worked themselves into a state of nervous exhaustion as they try, desperately, to scale all the targets the Forwardthinkorium sets up for them in the hope of shutting them the hell up, only to realise that another one always rises up ahead, like a 400 metre hurdle race that turns out to be an infinity metre hurdle race. You find a boyfriend, the Forwardthinkorium wants to know when the wedding is. The wedding takes place, the Forwardthinkorium wants to know when the conception is happening. The baby arrives, the Forwardthinkorium wants to know when you are going back to work. You go back to work, the Forwardthinkorium wants to know when you are going to have a second child. And put them down for school. And buy a house. And move to the country. And retire. And die.

Earthlings do not like this form of questioning, particularly if they are of an Anglo Saxon background. The skin of an Anglo Saxon earthling is very pink and tender and therefore has a much greater sensitivity to what they believe to be personal intrusions (American earthlings mind these much less thanks to their well-developed thorny outer hide, allowing them to talk about even their most embarrassing problems with total strangers and, ideally, on TV). Indeed, to the earthling, this form of small talk sounds not just intrusive but like an insinuation that there is something lacking in the earthling's present.

A small minority of Forwardthinkoriums do have a less than wholly benevolent intention behind their rat-a-tat-tat questioning – namely, a desire to alleviate the boredom of their own lives by finding out what's going on with yours. These Forwardthinkoriums are pitiable creatures and no more worth getting cross about than the weather. Instead, be charitable and offer up answers that will keep them buzzing for weeks:

'I'm not actually going to have a baby. I'm going to have giraffe. I've put my name down for a revolutionary new zoological scheme that impregnates you with animal sperm. Sure, I'll have to get the ceilings raised but apparently the birth is much easier.'

'I don't believe in marriage. Instead, we're going to have a public mating ritual in which we have sex in front of all our friends. It's just a really special moment – you should come along seeing as you are clearly so fascinated by our sex life.'

But in the main, Forwardthinkoriums don't have any interest in you or your life at all. This is just their default form of communication when they can't think of anything else to say. True, it is bad luck that their form of small talk is not only of so little interest to the speaker but often incredibly irritating to the listener, but this is not their fault, it's in their blood. So don't be horrid about them behind their backs and don't, most of all, mistranslate the constant prodding as an attack on you. They are just verbally drumming their fingers, not intentionally driving a bayonet through all your most sensitive neuroses.

So instead, make a tinkling laugh and give their hands an understanding pat. Touch them in the right spot and you can still feel the claw beneath the skin.

How to cheer up your friend who is depressed about being single without lying to them, patronising them or making them feel even worse

One has to begin by making the – I hope – patently obvious statement that there is nothing wrong with being single. Contrary to what movies, books and the world in general seem to think, being in a relationship is not the be-all and end-all of life, the only achievement that actually counts. Just because someone is in a relationship does not mean that they are smarter, sexier and all-round better than someone who is not, and if anyone ever makes you doubt that truth, counter it sharply with this argument-stopping fact: Stalin had girlfriends.

If finding happiness, fulfilment and equal companionship are probably among most people's ideals, not only do you not need to be in a relationship to achieve any of those but being in a relationship does not in any way guarantee them. It should also go without saying that being in a relationship is no bar to loneliness and it is more than possible to feel lonely when there is someone else sitting on the sofa with you. However, our subject today is single loneliness and if we try to tackle all forms of loneliness we'll never get to the point, or even out of this paragraph.

Equally, being single is often awesome. You can leave a party when you want to, whether that be 9 p.m. or 9 a.m.; you don't have to live in fear of ever hearing yourself described as 'my better half'; and you can spend all day lying on the sofa in your pyjamas watching *Murder She Wrote* and eating peanut butter straight out of the jar without seeing an expression of nausea on the face of the person who has regular sex with you. In short, look up all the examples the *Daily Mail* uses to prove single people are 'selfish' and substitute the word 'awesome'.

Nonetheless, there are times when being single can be tough. A person might have been happily single for years, and then one day, for whatever reason, they wake up and the misery goggles are on, skewing their entire view of their own life. Where once staying in and cooking a lovely meal for yourself was a delicious, peaceful treat, now you can only see how all recipes in cookbooks are measured out for two or four people and you end up having a half-hour tearful argument with yourself in the kitchen about whether that means you should just use half an onion as opposed to the whole onion the recipe specifies as it is just you who will be eating the meal and not the happy, normal couple with the amazing sex life that the cookbook is expecting. Just you, you, all alone you.

It's easy to have a sense of embarrassment about having feelings of single sadness. After all, you know – as may have been mentioned elsewhere in this book once or seven times – that the marriage ending is not the only happy ending available to a woman and therefore to admit to feeling the lack of a relationship can seem like a weak failure, a shamefully retro display of neediness, a pathetic stereotype crying out for comparisons to Bridget Jones. This, of course, is nonsense. Just because being with someone is not a woman's only option in life and shouldn't be her only focus, that doesn't mean it's some kind of self-betrayal to want it to be part of one's life. In any case, it is extremely unfair that Helen Fielding's book, which is one of the best comic novels ever written, has been diminished by lazy journalists and the far inferior copycat books that appeared in its wake as being shorthand for 'sad, desperate, baby-hungry women'. Similarly, it is deeply unfortunate that chick lit, a genre of literature that pretty much exists purely to talk about and universalise that very real sense of single loneliness, has actually reduced it to a shallow and vague cliché.

Speaking of loneliness, that often plays a major part in the feeling of single sadness, at least as much as the sense of a lack of a relationship, and loneliness can feel even more difficult to admit to. 'Taboo' is such an overused term I often wish it were a taboo in itself but admissions of loneliness really are something of a modern-day taboo. Jesus, don't you have anyone to friend on Facebook? (Incidentally, taking a slight aside, it is only when one is, at the very least, bored and quite possibly lonely with it that one has time to skitter around on Facebook, and if going to see a romcom when you're feeling lonely is often like squirting ammonia in your eye, then mooching on Facebook is like reaching for the cyanide. Even though a part of your brain knows that people present only a small sliver of their lives on Facebook, and that the Facebook representation of these lives bears as close a relation to the reality as a glossy advert in a magazine does to the actual product, there are few things more depressing than sitting on one's own and looking at photos of other people's fabulous, glamorous, friended-up lives. And no matter how many times you tell yourself that you know you're only seeing photos of the two weeks of the year they went on holiday to the Bahamas and not the many, many hours that they, too, were sitting around at home, similarly bored and looking at Facebook, the consolation is small.)

So if your single friend admits to feelings of slight loneliness, you are likely to be seeing just the ripple on the surface of a dark and murky swamp. As I said, it takes a lot of courage to admit to feelings of single-induced loneliness, and that your friend has come to you proves how much they value and trust you. Thus, your first reaction should be extreme flattery. And your next reaction should be complete panic that you don't let them down and say something that will traumatise them for ever.

Now, a simple fact that is often overlooked is it is not just women who feel occasionally lonely but – shockingly – men, too. Just because we don't actually see Mark Darcy moping around his giant house, singing along to Air Supply while staring down the maw of nihilistic despair in *Bridget Jones's Diary* doesn't mean he never does. And so, for purposes of gender equality, basic truth and simple shorthand, I shall give our hypothetical lonely single friend the pansexual name of 'Charlie'.

So Charlie calls you and the following conversation transpires:

> **Charlie:** Yeah, so, um, I guess I've been feeling a little down recently because I feel like I'm the only one of my friends who's not in a relationship and I know being in a relationship isn't the most important thing in the world but, um, I guess I've been feeling so lonely recently.

You: Oh honey, don't worry. Look [name of your partner] and I will come and meet you for a drink right now, OK? Or just come over here – the hubster and I are having a lazy Sunday and would love to see you!

You've failed before you've even begun. Look, if there's one thing worse than feeling single and lonely it's feeling single, lonely and outnumbered. I don't care how much Charlie likes (or claims to like) your partner – that is irrelevant.

When a friend is feeling lonely, they need one-on-one attention. They do not need you – and I'm sure this is not how you intended it but, in Charlie's state of mind, this is how it will be perceived – and your perfect relationship sitting opposite them, emanating couple smuggery as you occasionally give each little knee rubs and reassuring shoulder squeezes which are blatantly code for 'Don't worry, darling. I'll never let you be in the miserable state Charlie's in now. We're safe. Shall we go home now and have sex or is it too soon after our mammoth morning sesh?'

Why on earth would you bring your partner with you anyway? When a friend asks to see you, lonely or not, they mean you in the singular unless otherwise specified. You may not live in France but unless a friend specifically says, 'You and [name of partner]', they mean '*tu*', not '*vous*'. Although 'couple' and 'conjoined twins' may both begin with the same two letters, they are very different entities, particularly so to your friends. You do not need to bring your partner out with you all the time, let alone refer to him as 'the hubster' or whatever godawful term is the female equivalent.*
Remember, no matter how much your friends say they like

---

* 'Little lady'.

your partner, they, unlike you, are not in love with your partner. And that, frankly, is a damn good thing.

Sample conversation two:

> **Charlie:** I'm so down. I don't want to die alone.

> **You:** You won't die alone, I promise. You're too amazing for that.

WRONG! Unless your daily look is a turban patterned with little Saturns and stars, this is absolutely the wrong response. You are not psychic and HOPING that Charlie doesn't die alone is not the same as KNOWING it will not happen, and while you momentarily may not know the difference, Charlie definitely does. Lying is never a good idea, or at least not if the other person knows you're lying, and making promises you can't actually keep is not the reassurance Charlie needs.

But if your first sentence here is untrue, your second one is very, very wrong. It suggests that being in a relationship is like winning a beauty pageant and the unwitting intimation here is that Charlie's current single status is somehow a reflection on Charlie when it is, of course, actually a reflection on everyone else for not recognising Charlie's fabulousness. Worse, if you do say the above misguided comment, Charlie's tearful inner and quite possibly outer response to your comment is guaranteed to be 'If I'm so amazing, why am I alone?' Just thinking this will make Charlie feel even more of a cliché and, as a result, even worse. So, not helpful.

Third sample conversation:

Charlie: I'm so fed up with being single. I dread the weekends.

You: But so do I, Charlie! At least you don't have to spend your weekends with [insert the name of your partner here]'s parents, like I do! God, if I have to spend one more Sunday hearing his dad talk about the bloody cricket I will literally eat him to make him shut up.

This is pretty much akin to consoling a friend who just found out that they are infertile by whining about how much your twins cry when they haven't had their nap. It is cruel – unintentionally, sure, but still cruel. Competitive misery ('I have a cold.' 'Have you seen how sore my throat is? I WISH I had a cold!') is never an attractive quality in a person. Maybe you're the kind of person who likes to feel that you're always suffering the most; if so stop it because it's annoying. More likely you think you're making someone feel better by telling them that not only their misery has company but a whole party. This tactic does not work. It doesn't make anyone feel better. It makes them irritated. To insinuate that Charlie's concept of what being in a relationship is like is childishly idealistic is really not going to help. For a start, Charlie is not saying being in a relationship is perfect but rather that being alone is, at this moment, very hard, which is not only different but deserves a better response than a condescending dismissal.

You might think that you're helping with this reminder that all situations have their downsides, but it is the rare person who tells someone that they're not feeling so hot right now in the hope that the other person will start talking about their problems. They want to talk about THEIR problems, and, as their friend, it is your job to listen and to take their problems seriously.

Fourth sample conversation:

Charlie: I'm just so tired of being the only single person among my group of friends. Everyone's getting married and having babies and I'm always the fifth person on a table of five.

You: Is there no one in your office? Have you considered internet dating?

What is wrong with you? If you think Charlie is so stupid, why are you friends in the first place? I am pretty sure that Charlie has had a good look around the office already and as for internet dating, asking a single person if they have considered it is like asking someone where was the last place they saw their car keys. Maybe some people have not heard of internet dating – rare tribespeople in South America, time-travellers from the past – but it is extremely likely that your single friend has and for various reasons rejected the possibility. These reasons might include that, for every one story they hear about a friend of a friend of a friend meeting their future spouse on the internet, they've heard about 276 stories about someone's internet date announcing by way of introduction that they have chlamydia.

It is a tragic comment on the state of human development that so many people still don't understand that when someone comes to whinge to you, they don't actually want advice about how they could do things better – they just want to whinge. This applies to whinges about bad traffic one has just endured ('You know, you really should have taken the slip roads …') and it applies to loneliness. Most people's instinctive response to a friend whingeing is to present a solution that they think will fix the problem and make the friend feel better, but the one thing that will make the friend actually feel better is you listening and making sympathetic noises. That's it.

The exception to this rule in the case of the depressed single friend* is if YOU have something that you can do to fix the situation such as, say, a lovely single friend with whom you will fix up Charlie. Conversely, if you don't have anyone with whom to fix up Charlie, unless you think lemon juice is a great remedy for a paper cut, do not say, 'Oh, I wish I could help but I literally do not know any single people, everyone I know is an old married person like me these days, etc. etc.' It's bad enough feeling single and lonely without feeling like the last single and lonely person on planet Earth.

Conversely, telling Charlie that you know tonnes of people in the same position does not help, either. Charlie does not want to know that this current feeling of sadness might not just be the norm but also without end. So in short, don't talk about all the other single people you do or don't know, unless you are going to fix up Charlie with one of them. Other than that, just focus on your friend.

---

* The Case of the Depressed Single Friend: a heretofore unpublished Sherlock Holmes mystery, featuring boxes of chocolate that get mysteriously eaten overnight and hours lost upon social media websites.

Fifth sample conversation:

> **Charlie:** I'm just so tired of being on my own. I wish there was someone in my life.

> **You:** But Charlie, it's better to be on your own than with someone you don't love.

Shut. Up. This is certainly true, but if you yourself are in a happy relationship as you proffer this point, while I'm sure Charlie is very happy for you, and Charlie wants nothing but the best for you, Charlie now wants to plunge a Biro into your head. Charlie has not expressed a desire to be in a relationship for the sake of being in a relationship; Charlie has expressed feelings of loneliness. Charlie did not say 'I want to be with ANYone,' Charlie said, 'I want to be with SOMEone.' Thus, to say that Charlie is better off than being in an unhappy relationship is completely irrelevant and almost mean, really. You are essentially saying that Charlie's choice is between being alone or being in a loveless relationship, and that's a pretty unfair choice, not to mention an untrue one. After all, why should Charlie not have what you have?

Sixth sample conversation:

> **Charlie:** It just feels like all social occasions are couples-based now and I'm always the odd one out or even excluded.

You: Hey, you're right – couples do tend to hang out with other couples. Let's have a girls'/boys' night out! I haven't had one of those for ages!

Kicking off with what sounds very much like confirmation that there is a private members club from which Charlie has been excluded is not a good start. Nor is it particularly helpful to suggest that a single-sex social outing would be some kind of adorable novelty for you, like a slumber party, one you have long since outgrown because you're now too busy throwing grown-up dinner parties with all your mutual coupled-up sophisticated friends who keep the table numbers even and discuss dinner party things like catchment areas and the works of Stephen Poliakoff.

Charlie hasn't turned Orthodox and therefore can't mix with the opposite sex without the employment of a sheet with a hole in the middle; Charlie is just single. So you don't need to suggest single-sex outings, as though Charlie is now officially unfit for consumption by the other gender – just not outings that only include couples. There is a middle way between coupled-up-ness and segregation.

Look, it's actually not very hard to say the right thing to your depressed single friend; you just have to put a little thought into it and not spew out all the above clichés you've heard from movies and your mother. Jettison any idea that being single is a reflection on the single person. Instead, think carefully about why Charlie is single and why you are friends with Charlie and whether the two issues are related. Chances are, Charlie is a pretty special person, and therein lies your answer to both questions and your kicking-off point for your advice to Charlie. Every friend and every friendship is different so the conversation below should be taken as a template as opposed to a rule. But it's better than any of the above and might not just cheer up your friend but also preserve your friendship:

'Charlie, I'm so sad to see you so sad. I hadn't realised how lonely you were feeling because you have so many friends who love you. But of course, having friends is not the same as being in a relationship, if that's what you now want. Unfortunately for you, you're great. Awesome, even. Therefore it's harder for you to find someone to be with. You are not the type of person who just wants to be in a generic, soul-destroying relationship that ends up with the two of you getting married purely out of boredom, barely speaking to one another and having joyless affairs with other people. You want someone who you really connect with. And as you're so great, there are fewer people out there who are worthy of or even able to achieve that connection with you. They are out there, there are just fewer of them, and it takes patience and courage to find them, and while it is a sad reflection on the rest of the world how long it takes to find such a person, it is not a bad reflection on you. If anything, it is the reverse, and anyone who makes you feel bad about not being in a relationship is almost certainly in one of the aforementioned joyless ones and just trying to find self-vindication for their bad choice by making you feel insecure. These people are morons and you are a million times better than them. I hope you know that you really can call me any time and I always love hanging out with you. Please don't ever imagine that you are bothering me because I feel lucky that someone as great as you has chosen to be friends with me and I do believe that one day you will find the person who is lucky and great enough for you to want to be more than friends with them. Now, what time is it? Eleven a.m.? Perfect – cocktail time.'

Exercise – it's just like sex!

Have you ever noted the frequency with which advertisements for gyms make the possibly not scientifically proven connection between exercising and getting laid more* and felt a deep sense of despair at the way sex is now used to advertise everything – literally*2 everything,*3 I said*4 – and wept at the lack of creativity in the advertising industry?*5,*6

---

* David Barton gyms: 'Look better naked'; Equinox: photos by self-confessed 'pervert', Terry Richardson, of people making out with nary an exercise bike in sight.

*2 Dita von Teese stripping off to advertise a Renault Clio, for reasons not totally explained.

*3 A naked woman sitting next to a Samsung SF Notebook, again, for reasons not totally obvious.

*4 Every male deodorant and aftershave ever produced.

*5 'Here is the ultimate television commercial: here's the woman's face – beautiful. Camera pulls back – naked breasts. Camera pulls back – she's totally naked. Legs apart, two fingers right here, and it just says, "Drink Coke"', Bill Hicks.

*6 'By the way, if anyone here is in marketing or advertising, kill yourself,' Bill Hicks.

Or maybe you felt pity for the poor gyms at the insinuation that they are the slutty social outcasts of the high street: everyone avoids them and they can only entice people with pathetic promises of sexual favours?

Well, whatever your reaction, prepare to feel foolish because these adverts aren't saying going to the gym will get you more sex. They are saying that going to the gym is exactly – EXACTLY – like having sex. And they're right!

For a start, everyone talks about going to the gym a helluva lot more than they actually go to the gym – just like sex!

Most people who have never gone to the gym imagine it to be an experience that is, at best, physically awkward and, at worst, humiliating, but with potentially amazing rewards at the end – sex!

Magazines are obsessed with female celebrities' exercise regimes and whether they get up to any secretly away from the gaze of the paparazzi – sex sex sex!

In fact, the word 'sex' was derived from the word 'exercise', as a simple rearrangement of its letters makes clear (the remaining letters, I, C, E, E, R, spell, of course, 'I ceer' which is Greek for 'I talk a lot about').

It is a given in popular culture that both activities are an essential part of a modern person's weekly and ideally daily life which in turn has birthed many a misplaced insecurity. This has worked out to be rather lucrative for various industries, from porn magnates to sellers of gym memberships, both of whom peddle fantasies of the physical ideal and a surreally heightened lifestyle. Indeed, not only are whole magazines devoted to the subjects but it is the rare magazine that does not include at least one article on one or other subject, usually featuring 'insider tips' on how to become better and more effective at said pursuit. This in turn has fetishised these humble, even basic human activities into becoming symbols of aspiration and self-validation, when most people would prefer magazines and pop culture in general to stop going on about them quite so much and let them get on with these activities and their lives in general in peace.

The similarities extend well beyond the general to the particular. To wit, the first time you engage in either of these activities your thoughts will run through the following gamut:

Wow, look at me! Never thought I would finally get round to doing this – I'm a grown-up now!

Hey, I can do this! I can totally do this! I can't believe I was so worried beforehand.

Really? This is what everyone's been going on about all this time?

OK, I need a towel.

You will also have the reassuring realisation that, contrary to what you'd always feared, in real life no one laughs at how badly you imagine you're doing it. In fact, no one seems to be focusing on you at all because they're all so focused on how they're doing it themselves. And because they're half watching the TV.

This then leads to the next epiphany that the depiction of people doing this activity in movies and on TV bears pretty much no relation whatsoever to what it's like in real life. Depending on your gymnastic skills, this will come as either a relief or disappointment.

One definite disappointment in the disparity between the factual actions and fictional depictions is that you don't appear to burn half as many calories doing this as you were promised by those articles in women's magazines that list how many calories a woman burns doing various things, such as hoovering, shopping and having sex, these being the activities that make up an average woman's day (according to the magazines, which have apparently just arrived in town from the 1950s).

Make sure that you have all the kit within easy reach because it really is a bit of a drag to pause mid-proceedings to fetch an essential from across the room. However, you don't need as much kit as advertisers might have led you to believe. In fact, too much kit is merely a distraction and there is a direct correlation between how much people spend on paraphernalia and how little of the activity they actually do. But whatever kit you do need, bring it, because I guarantee that no one else will have it, or at least they'll claim they don't.

Contrary to what anyone says, water breaks are definitely allowed.

Speaking of other people, some of them will take great care about their hygiene: wiping off all surfaces beforehand, frequent wipes with a towel, and so on. Others just go for it, sweat flying everywhere without a care, germs of previous occupants be damned. It's really a matter of personal preference but, no matter which approach you take, do take the necessary precautions not to catch anything nasty from the experience.

Afterwards, every time, you will think about how amazing you now feel and that you gotta make this part of your daily routine. It is highly likely, though, that it will then be a long time – a surprisingly long time, even – before you do it again.

And finally, always go to the bathroom beforehand.

How to read women's magazines without wanting to grow a penis

Hadley Freeman walks into the restaurant, a mere ten minutes late which makes her practically early in celebrity terms. Everyone, of course, looks up as she walks past, gliding effortlessly in her five-inch Louboutins but dressed, otherwise, low key and casual in a Céline trench coat, last season's Prada dress and carrying an enviable orange Birkin bag. The maître d' immediately hovers into view but she insists that he make no fuss and graciously refuses his offer of a free glass of champagne as she slips into the banquette next to me.

'Just water, thanks.' She smiles at him before whispering conspiratorially to me, 'Must keep rehydrated, you know!'

She's smaller in person than I expected, celebrity regulation-sized tiny, and her face looks defiantly, bravely un-Botoxed judging from the crinkles around her eyes. But that extraordinary beauty is unmistakable, like something from another era. A more beautiful era.

'I'm so sorry – I do hope I haven't kept you waiting too long,' she says anxiously, turning those famous liquid chocolate eyes upon me and biting that plump lower lip that has entire websites dedicated to its wonders.

I assure her she has not and she flashes that 100-watt smile in relief and turns back to the menu before alighting triumphantly on something that takes her fancy.

'Let's have some scones, shall we?' she suggests. 'After all, isn't that what one is supposed to have for tea?'

Giggling naughtily, we agree to carb-load and as soon as they arrive ('Thank you.' She smiles up at the waiter who then nearly faints dead away) she tucks into the scones hungrily, trowelling on the butter and cream without a second thought although how on earth she fits them into her tiny physique must rank as the eighth wonder of the world.

'So you wanted to talk to me about women's magazines, right?' she asks, scones finished, pushing her hand through her newly cropped locks ('I had them cut for a part – I just feel so free with short hair,' she exclusively reveals).

Yes, exactly, I nod, about why they are so annoying and yet why so many women read them even though they know how annoying they are. And as you have spent approximately 93 per cent of your waking hours reading women's magazines, Hadley, you seemed like the person to talk to about this.

'Well, certainly the sycophantic celebrity interviews that dominate so many of these magazines don't help their cause. You know the ones: in which the female celebrity is described so gushingly it would make a Mills and Boon writer blush, in which her celebrity status is seen as an indication of her inherent superiority to the human race and any indication that she is slightly lower maintenance than Imelda Marcos and more polite than Alan Sugar is taken as proof that she is the reincarnation of Mother Teresa. Oh THANK YOU,' she says sweetly to the waiter as he clears away the remnants of our scones and he nearly faints dead away.

But to be fair, those interviews aren't limited to women's magazines – one finds them in pretty much all glossy magazines, right?

'True, but what's interesting – by which I mean irritating, of course – about them in women's magazines is the way they are loaded down with what women's magazine editors describe as "feminine anecdotes" – you know the kind.' She sighs, twirling her glossy hair around a manicured finger and criss-crossing her endless legs. 'How incredibly perfect-looking she is; how marriage has changed her life; how motherhood has changed her life or, if she hasn't had children, why not; what designers the celebrity likes; how thin she is; what she eats; how much she loves clothes; how she secretly loves to cook; how she loves her boyfriend but really adores her girlfriends, how she and the journalist are now best friends, etc., etc. And every time the celebrity shows any sign of an unfeminine characteristic – confidence, ambition, bolshiness – this is then tempered with an assurance that she also really likes make-up and has plenty of insecurities, too. It's basically about reinforcing all the most tedious and conventional clichés about women – yet in a magazine for women.'

She sighs again crossly but smiles prettily at the end. While she is clearly certain in her opinion on the subject it's also obvious from her warmth that at the end of the day she's a real girl's girl. I notice her fiddling a little with rings on her fingers, an endearing habit suggesting shyness, or maybe a subliminal desire to be married. She has always been very private about her love life but there have been recent rumours that she is currently dating P. Diddy.

So women's magazines are adulatory about women? That doesn't sound so bad, I suggest.

'No, they aren't at all,' she replies, her hands smoothing over her slightly bulging but still barren tummy. 'In fact, it's extraordinary how many women's magazines make being a woman sound utterly awful, mainly that we're all always at war … with ourselves! We love chocolate – but we don't want to be fat! We love celebrities – but we envy their perfect lives! We love fashion – but it's so expensive! Gah! It's such a brain-splitting nightmare being a woman, no wonder we all have to binge on chocolate ice cream every night to cope with the strain.'

This seems an odd activity to cite. Perhaps Hadley, despite her apparently perfect life and tendency to rant on a bit, binges at night on ice cream, eating away her insecurities. And which of us girls doesn't do that occasionally?

'And this brings me to another problem with women's magazines: a lot of them don't seem to like women very much. That women are subjected to a much higher level of scrutiny about their physical appearance than men is so well known it's a truism. But,' she continues, fiddling with her dress which is just that little bit too snug around the hips, 'it seems downright perverse for women's magazines to perpetuate this prejudice, particularly in celebrity gossip magazines aimed at women with all their guff about who's fat, who's lost weight, who's seeing who and who's just been dumped, reducing women to nothing but cellulite and vaginas. After all, I'm assuming you don't see long-shot photos in *Saga* magazine of Judi Dench with accompanying copy snickering at how decrepit she's looking. Women's magazines should make women feel good about themselves, not laugh at one another.'

Well, that certainly makes the adulatory celebrity interviews sound preferable, I venture.

'Yes and no – oh THANK YOU,' she says, looking up to the waiter when he brings over a pot of tea, and he nearly faints dead away. 'Because ultimately the message is the same: women have to be perfect. Either they're these extraordinary celebrity creatures whose every move is downright angelic, or they're tubby lards who dare to be spotted via a long lens with a less than flat tummy. But I think you need to differentiate between the various kinds of women's magazines. First, there are the celebrity gossip magazines which, for whatever reason, are seen as women's magazines.'

That's because the menfolk are too busy reading manly things, like Michael Lewis and Andy McNab books. Money and guns – that's what the menfolk like! Men aren't the least bit interested in celebrities. Just like how they're not interested in clothes. Those are women's things. Everyone knows that, I explain.

'Clearly. Celebrity gossip magazines have been around for as long as celebrities, stuffed with curiously in-the-know stories from suspiciously unidentified sources.'

Presumably these sources are close and intimate friends of the celebrities – that's how they know the stories.

'Maybe. Or it could be because "source" is Latin for "the celebrity's PR trying to keep his client in the news" or possibly Greek for "the journalist who is pulling stories and conjectures out of his ass because he is on a desperate deadline". All women's magazines have an element of celebrity to them but to be a proper celebrity magazine, to use something of an oxymoron, the magazine has to be composed largely of these unattributed pieces of gossip and feature a paparazzi shot on the cover of a photogenic female celebrity, looking startled and allegedly going through a difficult time in her personal life. In the 1990s a black and white Peter Crawford photo of Evangelista, Turlington, Campbell, Patitz and Crawford was the iconic women's magazine cover; in the 2010s, it will probably be a long-lens shot of an unhappy-looking Katie Holmes walking out of Whole Foods.'

Poor brave Katie. She really is such an inspiration, isn't she?

'Yes, to ex-wives of sofa jumpers everywhere. Then you have the fashion magazines that focus almost entirely on fashion – happy to have cleared that up for you. And finally, you have the features magazines that are built around features articles aimed at very specific demographics, from 1980s Sloanes (*Tatler*) to self-help junkies (*Psychologies*), from anachronistic sex addicts (*Cosmopolitan*) to people who want to know about the Rwandan disaster but also care deeply about which bikinis suit pear-shaped bodies (*Marie Claire*). Ah, woman: such a multi-layered subtle mystery, she.'

She stops suddenly, apparently thinking while tucking another lock of chestnut hair behind her ear. Perhaps she has realised how much she's been ranting away and is suddenly embarrassed. I think she is.

'Would you like any more tea, madam?' the waiter, suddenly hovering into view, asks.

'Mmm, just a Diet Coke – THANK YOU,' she replies, and the waiter nearly faints dead away.

Well, it sounds like you really hate women's magazines, Hadley, I suggest.

'No, no, not at all!' she cries, holding up a perfectly manicured hand bedecked with Kenneth Lane rings. 'That's not it at all. If I hated women's magazines I just wouldn't care about them. I love them, but not all of them are created equal. I definitely hate the ones that make women feel bad about themselves as that is clearly the opposite of what a women's magazine should do. I'm not saying a women's magazine should be like some kind of self-help cheerleader, all "you go, girl!" nonsense, as that's just annoying. But it shouldn't make you want to head off to a sex change clinic so that you are no longer part of the demographic at which the magazine is aimed. At their worst, women's magazines are too lazy to think outside the usual conventions of how the media talk about women and to women and so appear dated and mean. They are riddled with lazy clichés churned out by journalists petrified into paralysis of doing anything that might lead to their falling circulations plummeting any further. Therefore, they consist of a merry-go-round of features that go a little something like this: weight-motherhood-relationships-celebrities-weight-motherhood-relationships-celebrities. That is definitely not the case with all women's magazines, but it is true of some of them.

'Yet I do think that some of the negative reactions readers occasionally have to women's magazines stem from not understanding them properly. For example, I suspect a lot of people feel patronised by them and wonder why women's magazines talk to their readers as if they were mentally subnormal, with their silly sycophantic interviews and their plugging of products that clearly no one reads. But what you have to understand is that a lot of women's magazines aren't actually written for women – they're written for celebrity PRs and advertisers. The interviews are so sycophantic because the commissioning editors have to reassure all the celebrity PRs out there that their clients won't be asked anything more taxing than why they recently cut their hair and what their birthstone is (emerald, by the way). This then ensures that the magazine will always have a celebrity interview to put on the cover because magazine editors believe, rightly or wrongly, it is more important to have a celebrity cover than it is to have any journalistic integrity as they think that women will buy a magazine because of the cover star – but they probably won't actually read the interview because, really, who has time to read a 1,500-word interview these days?

'As for the advertising, that's obvious. Women's magazines will always be slavering in adulation about any fashion or cosmetic label and trend because they need to keep those companies' advertising accounts. So while, as a reader, it might seem that a magazine is treating you like a moron when it urges you to buy such "essential" things as an "Anti-ageing, time-reversing, dermatological epidermis renewal crème, £175", it's not. Such advice has nothing to do with you at all. It's entirely to do with the advertising accounts, and while this is irritating and doesn't make for very interesting reading, at least you're not being deliberately insulted. Incidentally, I use Hydra Life Pro Youth Light Refracting Intense Deep Hydration Sorbet Cream. It's literally changed my face. Literally,' she says, gently patting her very real but completely perfect complexion.

'We know that the majority of magazines aimed at women are completely stupid – yet they sell millions of copies a month,' she continues, tapping her lipsticked mouth thoughtfully. 'So the question, I guess, is why, and it's something I as a reader have sometimes wondered when I see the stack of magazines I buy every month piled up in the corner of my living room.' She makes another tinkling laugh.

'Reading a celebrity magazine can feel especially hard to justify to oneself, on moral and intellectual grounds. While it might not be up there with ripping a baby calf away from its mother mid-suckle in order to feast on its still beating heart, there comes a point in most magazine readers' lives when you find yourself looking at another pap shot of a celebrity's traumatised child (and probable future drug-addicted reality TV star) and you have to ask yourself, Who am I and WHAT am I doing looking at this?

'Any publication that features paparazzi shots of children should be shunned. They are the journalism equivalent of high street stores that rely on Indian sweatshops in that they are exploiting children – children – for their own financial benefit. For a similar reason, any celebrity who encourages photographers to take pictures of their children should be treated with a hefty scoop of scepticism simply because being in the public spotlight makes it that much harder to have a healthy and happy childhood.

'But child-exploiting paparazzi and any publications that are predicated solely on talking about female celebrities' body shape and love lives aside, celebrity magazines themselves are, really, utterly harmless, even if it may cause a smart woman some consternation as to why she is reading them. Come on, the smart woman asks herself with exasperation as she eagerly forks out £1.25 in the newsagent, why on earth do you CARE about Jen's newest beachside retreat, Kate's new Manhattan life, Victoria's new favourite designer? The answer is, you don't. You do, however, care about stories, and this leads me to explaining why celebrity magazines are like Charles Dickens.

'When I was at school and forced to study Charles Dickens I took two lessons away from the experience: 1. that the parodies of Dickens ("Oh larks, Mrs Scrumpybum, do you mean to say that this mysterious old man is secretly my father? And this blonde orphanness will be my future bride? And I have suddenly come into an unexpected fortune? Oh, Mrs Scrumpybum!") are nigh indistinguishable from the real thing; and 2. magazine readers in Dickens's day had it pretty damn good.

'Dickens's novels were originally published in serial in weekly and monthly magazines, mainly because people were much weaker in those days due to malnutrition and wouldn't have been able physically to hold door-stoppers like *Dombey and Son* in their feeble, rickety limbs. The public would get worked up into such piques of curiosity about Dickens that there would be hysterical crowds begging for the next instalment of the magazine, desperate to find out if Little Nell died (spoiler: yes), if Nancy died (spoiler: yes) and if Dora died (spoiler: yes).

'As my and everybody else's English GCSE teacher explained, these tales were the soap operas of that day, which is true, but they were also the celebrity gossip magazines of their day. Celebrity magazines aren't really about celebrities – they're about storylines enacted via the celebrities through the magazines, such as, what next for Kristen Stewart and Robert Pattison after she cheats on him? How is poorly Lindsay Lohan doing these days? And what – oh what? – will become of little Suri Cruise? These magazines are more artful than Dickens when it comes to constructing weekly cliffhangers out of what is, quite possibly, nothing other than a couple of fortuitous pap shots and an unnamed "source".

'I appreciate that it's perhaps not so much fun for the celebrities for their personal lives to be turned into plot lines in some kind of multi-stranded production of *Into the Woods*, but it does explain the appeal of these brainless publications for many brainy women. It's not about the celebrities – it's about the stories.'

And what about fashion magazines? I ask, going in for the hard-hitting question. I know you've written for those in your time. Can you justify those?

She nods earnestly. 'I have and I can and yes,' she continues, holding up that elegant manicured finger before I can interrupt, 'I am all too aware of their failings. The way these magazines venerate youth, thinness and wealth is inexcusable and, to be honest, baffling. Honestly, one doesn't have to be skinny to wear nice clothes and I speak from experience on that one.

'But I also find fashion magazines fascinating, really, because they exist so completely in their own weird little beautiful world and make absolutely no pretence about having any kind of connection with their readers, nor, to be honest, do they seem to care that much about what their readers do which is something of a rarity when it comes to the media and women. The vast majority of the time, the media tell women what to do, how to live their lives, when to have children and so on. Fashion magazines couldn't give a toss about any of that. They only care about Balenciaga's experimentation with waterfall hems this season and Yohji Yamamoto's high-heeled trainers. Some readers are offended by fashion shoots that feature extremely expensive clothes and think that the magazine is assuming that everyone has Aerin Lauder's bank account and will pop out on Saturday to buy a £6,500 Chanel dress. But this is to misunderstand fashion shoots. Fashion magazines aren't catalogues and they're not telling you to buy the clothes – they are far simpler and more narcissistic than that. Fashion magazines are literally just saying, "Look! Look at this dress! And this coat! And this shoe! Look! Look!" There is something in that simplicity that I like. It's like hanging out with your very shallow friend for an afternoon: you might not want to share a flat with her, but sometimes you do just want casual chitchat.'

We've been talking so long now the light outside has gone and the shadows are lengthening. But Hadley shows no sign of concern about the time. I think this means we're now best friends.

'Would you perhaps like a pre-dinner aperitif?' asks the waiter, hovering into view.

'Oh, that would be lovely – THANK YOU,' she replies, and the waiter nearly faints dead away.

'As for the features magazines, well, because these are such a broad church they generally represent the best and the worst of the women's magazine market. Some contain genuinely smart writing and interesting ideas that make readers feel part of an intimate female-only club, others are blatantly churned out when the commissioning editor's brain was on autopilot and they do nothing but reinforce old gender stereotypes and rehash stories that have been written a million times before (yes, please tell me once again about how moving to a picturesque foreign country was hard at first but ultimately rewarding – I CAN'T GET ENOUGH OF THAT).

'For whatever reason, some of my favourite women's magazines – ones that had great fashion and fantastic writing that felt like the vocalisation of my soul – did not last long in this world, such as *Nova* and *Minx*. Now if I want to read women's-oriented stories that feel immediately relevant to me written in a smart and funny voice, I don't go to the newsagent but head instead to the web for internet magazines and blogs, such as the Vagenda, Jezebel, the Hairpin, Feministing and so on. Maybe the internet is just the more natural medium for quick smarts as well as, obviously, immediacy.

'But look, you can't relax in the bath reading a blog – well, not without fear of electrocuting yourself, and that might undermine the relaxation element. All good people like to slob out occasionally, turn off their brains and just feel some glossy paper between their fingers. You don't always want *foie gras*, you know: sometimes only Pringles will do. In times like that, the hilarious and anachronistic magazine conventions can feel almost comforting, like when you go home to visit your parents and your mother makes that same comment about how you really should get highlights in your hair that she's been making since you were eighteen years old. Don't buy any magazines that perpetuate lame female stereotypes or in any way wreak havoc on children's mental wellbeing and don't buy any that make you feel unhappy or dissatisfied with your life. That's it, really. Otherwise, just lie back in the bath and enjoy the pap. Oh THANK YOU,' she says as the waiter hovers into view with our aperitifs, and he nearly faints dead away.

There will always be something wrong with your body, which means nothing is wrong with your body

Epiphanies are rare and beautiful things. James Joyce was uncommonly prone to them, or at least uncommonly prone to using them as a convenient plot device. Archimedes' bath-based one changed the world, and possibly also his relations with his neighbours when his bathwater started seeping through their ceiling. And I had one when someone told me about the term 'cunt bump'.

'A what?'

'A cunt bump,' he replied.

'I'm pretty sure you can get a cream for that,' I said.

'Have you really never heard that term before?'

'Uh, no.'

'Really? I read it years ago in some magazine.'

I used to quite like reading men's magazines for the same reason I occasionally take a different route home from work: it's nice to check out a parallel if surprisingly similar universe, and one that takes you eventually to the same destination. But after a while, I realised there were only so many times I could look at a fashion spread of 'this season's best satchel bags' or read another feature entitled 'Our

Exclusive Report from the Basel Watch Fair!' or 'Why Willem Dafoe is the Coolest Man in the World'.

So I'd missed this exciting new discovery, this conquering of a new land, the land of Cunt Bump. I enquired further and it seems that, according to the men's magazine world, when a woman stands in profile, there is a small rise – a hillock if you like – just before one gets to what one of my friends calls 'a woman's secret place'.

'You mean her stomach?' I asked my informant.

'No – it's hard. Like a bone.'

'You mean her pelvis?'

'Yeah, I guess.'

And that is when I had my epiphany. No, not that men's magazines are just as enthusiastic as their female counterparts at coining terms for heretofore under-discussed faults on a woman's body. Rather, there will always be something wrong with a woman's body. Therefore, nothing is wrong with a woman's body.

It's always interesting when someone overplays their hand. To quote Jennifer Aniston's last halfway memorable line, here comes the science bit.

To say that the beauty industry and women's magazines, instead of making women feel good about themselves as they claim to do, simply encourage insecurities for their own financial benefit is like complaining that banks, far from keeping our money safe, seem to be making a lot of money for themselves.

Which is not to say that even the most seasoned of us magazine readers and beauty product shoppers are not occasionally taken by surprise by the shameless venality of these industries. Recently I had to go to a department store to buy a tub of moisturiser for a friend of mine after my dog ate hers when she was looking after him. So on the downside, I had to spend $150 on a tub of carcinogenic chemicals and whale sperm (I think that's what the sales assistant said). On the plus side, my dog's digestive tract now looks about five years younger than it actually is, and that's thirty-five in dog years.

As I was paying for this gorgeously packaged modern-day snake oil, the sales assistant looked at me closely.

'You know, we have creams for discolouration,' she confided chummily.

'I'm sorry?' I said.

'Patches of discolouration, from sun damage. You see? Right here on your cheek. And here. Oh! And here. It's very ageing but I have a great cream that can help you with that. Only $275,' she explained, ever so sympathetically. Now, I have looked in the mirror many times in my life but never once had I noticed that I have a complexion like camouflage. Perhaps my displeasure showed beneath my discolouration because she swiftly switched tack from insulting to that other approach beloved of moisturiser sales assistants: all-inclusive girliness.

'We all get it!' she said sweetly, touching her own face. This approach might have been more reassuring if she wasn't about thirty years older than me. But seeing my face, discolouredly gawping, she surmised that I wasn't about to bite and so skipped to the financial conclusion of our relationship. 'Here's your receipt, sign here,' she added.

'So I take it the insult is included in the price?' I asked.

'What?'

'Never mind,' I huffed, stomped out with my moisturiser and my dignity, and then spent the rest of the evening in my bathroom, studying my face for discolouration.

For centuries, snake oil salesmen and their advertisers, aka magazines, have expended much energy telling women all about their physical faults which, interestingly, are often a natural part of being a woman but, nonetheless, faulty. And then, they prescribe remedies (allegedly) to fix these (alleged) problems.

But what happens when these sources then run out of problems to make women feel bad about themselves, I mean to make them spend money, I mean to sort out post-haste? After all, there are only so many times a magazine writer can hack out an article about what a woman should do if her stomach is less than flat, especially since they've marketed Spanx so effectively to the masses. There needs to be something new, some uncharted area on a woman's body that is, in some way, wrong, disgusting and possibly, at this moment, unfixable.

Also, don't 'flabby tummy' and 'thigh cellulite' sound a bit, well, dated at this point, like cottage cheese and calorie counting? I mean, we've been talking about them for years! We need a new body insecurity, something a bit trendier, a bit more zeitgeisty, a bit more, you know, NOW. But whatever could that be? Hello, cankles.

The term 'cankles' first came to my attention in 2005 but it took another four or so years for it to gain popularity, if not credibility, in the media. Yet as is always the way with something new, particularly when the new thing is imaginary, the public needed a little instruction into what it actually was that they were supposed to be seeing and fearing. Thankfully, the media were more than happy to oblige: 'Cankles occur when the calf meets the foot in one unapologetic union. It's a fusion of calf and ankle.'*

---

* 'As Cheryl Cole reveals hers, a fellow sufferer bemoans the curse of the cankles', *Daily Mail*, 25 May 2011.

181

Perhaps you'd always thought that the place where the calf met the foot was the ankle. Had the 'c' heretofore been silent and now we were supposed to pronounce it? Was this like the great Opal Fruits/Starburst switch of 1998?

But no. This was not a linguistic development but rather a biological one. It seemed, against all odds, that a new faulty part of the female physiognomy had been discovered, despite women's bodies having been, one might have thought, pretty closely studied already. But you know, people doubted Columbus when he found a new land so maybe cankles were the new America. As John Donne would doubtless pen had he not been so slack and died before this new unearthing, 'Oh your cankles, your newfound fault! How am I repulsed in discovering thee!'*

Most women have heard of thick ankles, which are generally something that afflicts older women and pregnant women, two demographics who, God knows, the media criticise plenty and among their many, many faults is that they offer limited fodder to make women who are not pregnant or over thirty-five feel bad about their bodies.

Or do they?

After all, one of the changes conception does to a woman's body is the thickening of the ankles. This – if you are a soulless magazine or tabloid newspaper writer whose entire career depends upon making women feel bad about themselves – is interesting because this is also one of the few physical signs of pregnancy that, while caused by pregnancy, has nothing to do with the pregnancy itself unlike, say, the swollen stomach and painful breasts. So wait a minute wait a

---

* With apologies to John Donne and his Elegy XX, 'To His Mistress Going to Bed'.

minute wait a gosh-darned minute! Maybe we can say that some women have these thick ankles too! And it's not caused by pregnancy, it's just the way they're built! And with that, the soi-disant journalist jumped out of his bath and went running down Fleet Street naked.

Lo, the narrative of cankles followed the usual path: tabloids and women's magazines discussed them; then used photos of celebrities to illustrate them (an essential part of discussing body insecurities, of course, is the ostensible suggestion that all women have problems so the reader shouldn't feel bad, but the actual inference is if even Helen Mirren is held up for criticism then what hope for you?); then ran first-person pieces about the 'hell' of having them.

So far, so status quo. Except for one big problem.

First, it seems unlikely that most people had heard anyone discussing the shapeliness or otherwise of a woman's ankles outside a Jane Austen novel, and the characters in those books apparently had so little to do that a good evening out would involve taking a 'turn around the room', so small wonder if they spent time sweating the small stuff.

But that wasn't the real problem with cankles. The real problem was that they don't exist.

Female celebrities running the talent gamut from Helen Mirren to Miley Cyrus, from Hillary Clinton to Cheryl Cole, were all cited by tabloids and magazines as sufferers of 'cankles', with Cole – a woman so tiny one needs a microscope to see her, let alone her ankles with or without the 'c' – coming in for some especial criticism ('Y'see, ladies! If even teeny tiny Cheryl can have them, NO ONE is safe! Constant vigilance and self-hatred is de rigueur!'). Yet no matter how many close-up photos were published of these women's cankles (sure, Clinton might broker some pretty impressive foreign relations but have you seen her ankles?), all that was visible to the naked, non-blind eye were, in fact, ankles. Not deformed ankles, not thick ankles – ankles.

Let me tell you something: when even an occasional fashion journalist can't see the problematic body issue, there is no problem.

Wait, scratch that: there was a problem but perhaps not the one that was suggested. In 2009 – the year of the rise of 'cankles', as chance would have it – Christian Louboutin designed a Barbie doll and he did more than put her in over-the-knee boots, known to shoe aficionados as Vivians in honour of the film character who will for ever be associated with that footwear: he finally sorted out Barbie's notorious fat ankles.

'She needed great shoes, a thinner ankle and, to me, because I'm obsessed with feet, a foot more curved,' Louboutin explained.*

As well as surprising those who'd perhaps thought it was a different part of Barbie's anatomy that was disproportionally oversized for the rest of her body, this comment suggested that Louboutin doesn't have a clue how a woman's foot should or even can look, which one might have thought would be a problem for a man whose career consists of designing shoes for women.

But before any of those feminist types started waving their hairy pitchforks, Louboutin was quick to clarify that he didn't mean that Barbie had fat ankles: 'Barbie's foot has always been shaped less "curvy" than the rest of her perfect

* 'Louboutin Fetes Barbie at 50', *Women's Wear Daily*, 16 October 2009.

body,' he said. 'I just added my little science to Barbie and I've been proud to serve her. But fat ankles she didn't have, she just could have had thinner ankles. That's all.'

Yes, that's all! She COULD have thinner ankles, just as she could have three arms, or she could have a second head. But really, one can't criticise Christian for having an unrealistic concept of how the human body works seeing as he himself manages such extraordinary feats with his own body, such as learning how to talk out of his ass.

I can't even be bothered to deal with what is almost a side note, Louboutin describing Barbie's body as 'perfect', because designers making stupid comments about what constitutes an ideal woman's body is pretty much up there in terms of easy media bait with models talking about how little they eat.

Yet for a designer – a shoe designer, no less – to say that Barbie's ankles needed a bit of slimming is a little different from Kate Moss saying, 'Nothing tastes as good as skinny feels,' which caused clutched-handkerchief outrage in the media at the time. Louboutin's claim that a doll whose already ridiculous body would be made more beautiful by being even more ridiculous suggests that at the very least he feels that a woman's body in its natural state is irredeemably faulty (which is not that surprising seeing as his entire career is based on hoiking women up on their tiptoes in the belief that their feet look better entirely vertical).

But that was just the opinion of some dozy French designer, I told myself, and making generalisations from his opinions would be like thinking *Vogue* is in any way representational of the real world.

And then I came up against the cunt bump. So to speak.

Being a perennial avoider of any activity that requires me to undress in a communal changing room, I do not have much experience when it comes to looking at women's naked bodies other than my own so I cannot say with iron-clad certainty whether some women protrude more than others in that certain place. But I do know this: when men's magazines are sniggering about the shape of a woman's skeleton above a place that they would be lucky to be acquainted with, we have gone past the point of merely monetising body insecurities to pretty much an open admission that what these folk don't like is, not extra bulges, extra hairs, extra lines: they don't like women.

One only needs to walk through a chemist these days to realise that at any point of the day there are about 317 things that are allegedly wrong with a woman: hairs where there should be only peachy flesh, flesh where there should only be air, air where there should be a perfumed fragrance. This is clearly at least as much about money as misogyny because these claims are made, not to make women miserable, but to make women spend money by making them miserable, and the order of those ambitions is important.

When you get to the base level of discussing bones, making coinages for non-existent problems, remodelling Barbie dolls and complaining about physical alterations that even the publications admit can't be remedied ('drooping knee skins can affect all body shapes and sizes ... many plastic surgeons advise against surgery. Knees are one of the hardest areas of the body to have done because there is nowhere to conceal the scarring'),* then we are in the area of full-on misogyny, because there is no money to be made from this.

---

* 'How Cindy Crawford's Knees Tell the Truth About her Age', *Daily Mail*, 6 October 2011.

While it is always alarming to encounter blatant hate speech, in this context it is actually quite liberating. There is always going to be something wrong with your body according to certain sectors because it is a grown-up woman's body. Therefore, there is nothing actually wrong with your body. In fact, your body is so great that they now have to make up things that don't even exist or look towards your skeletal structure to find something to complain about and, by doing so, they have gone just that little bit too far and ended up satirising themselves. And like all good satires, this one points to the truth: that underneath any article and any advert that suggests a woman should look like anything other than a human woman lies a hot and sticky swamp of misogyny. The constant criticism of the female body proves that its critics aren't trying to alter the female body – they just don't want a female body at all. It's like constantly criticising a cherry pie for being too sweet, too fruity, too crusty, too pie-y. Maybe, dude, you don't want a cherry pie. Maybe you want a peanut butter sandwich instead. And that is fine – go off and have a sandwich. But that pie is a pie and it will never be a sandwich, no matter how much you try to change it.

In the wake of what must unfortunately be referred to as a rash of penis photos in the first half of 2011 appearing on the internet, usually with a relatively well-known American face at the other end of it, the wonderful comedian Kristen Schaal was asked whether it's more acceptable for a woman to send naked photos of herself than it is for a man.

'The female body is beautiful,' she replied. 'Penises look like a species discovered living on the ocean floor near undersea sulfur jets.'*

---

* *The Daily Show*, 7 June 2011.

As much as I love Schaal, I try to avoid arguments that favour one thing at the pointless expense of something else. The female body is beautiful. Miraculous, really. And to be fair, the male body is very nice too, even if most of us would prefer not to see photos of the penises of various rappers* and footballers*2 if we're not actually sleeping with them.

This is why women of the world should thank daft tabloids, women's magazines, Christian Louboutin and everyone else who hates women's bodies: by acting as the extreme end of the female body obsession wedge, these groups have revealed the faultiness of the whole enterprise. Anyone who hates women's bodies can go play with their Barbie dolls.

---

* Kanye West.

*2 Brett Favre.

Beyond the armpit: a ten-point (plus three addenda and some posh little footnotes) guide to being a modern-day feminist

'Words cannot express the depth of gratitude we owe to those brave feminist foremothers who struggled and sacrificed, endured imprisonment and ridicule, and fought fearlessly to grant future generations of American women a voice' **Sarah Palin, 2010**

'I'm not a feminist – I hail men, I love men. I celebrate American male culture, beers, bars and muscle cars' **Lady Gaga, 2009**

I am going to take two things for granted here. First, I am going to assume that if you are holding this book and still reading it that you are smarter than Lady Gaga, who is able to take feminism's advances so much for granted that she thinks 'feminist' is a fancy term for 'beer-loathing, car-despising man-hater'. Or maybe she really doesn't like the concept of gender equality, in which case she is welcome to give back her right to vote as it could doubtless be used better elsewhere. And I am also going to assume that you are smarter than Sarah Palin who at least has some kind of concept that feminism means women being able to work and live freely, even if she doesn't quite get that this means giving all women full control over their own bodies in the form of sex education, contraception and abortion rights.

The reason I can take these two things as givens is because this book is primed to burst into flames when sullied by the hands and eyes of anyone of lesser intelligence than those two women. So if you are, in fact, now just making out these words on the charred remains of the few pages that survived, you should probably give it up. And maybe go sort out what's left of your hair.

As we've established that you are smarter than Palin and Gaga, chances are that you are a feminist and know that women are, of course, just as competent as men simply because if you have more than two brain cells it is medically impossible to believe that genitalia determine intelligence or capability. Yes, an organ does dictate whether one person is smarter than another, but this organ is the brain, not the penis.

However, being a feminist is not entirely straightforward these days. This might seem surprising because 'gender equality' is not, as long as you aren't Jim Davidson, a particularly difficult concept to grasp. Nonetheless, it is just absolutely shocking the way so many young girls out there who are wearing high heels and buying fashionable clothes and oh my God do you know how much money they spend on *%&^$^£%zzzzlknflrsngvlskedncvlkafnwsfklcnq-acswcsadv

Sorry, I think, I just fell asleep on the keboard. I mean, the keyboard. Apologies, the 'y' key was stuck to m forehead. I mean, my forehead.

'Being a feminist is not entirely straightforward' does not mean 'let's rehash that unbelievably tedious 1995 debate about whether high heels or "fuck me shoes" are incompatible with feminism', or whether it's calling them 'fuck me shoes' that's incompatible with feminism, partly because it is very boring and mainly because it results in women on the same side beating up on each other to no purpose at all. This is a classic example of something called 'doing the other side's work for them'.

Yet as I said, being a feminist can be a little tricky because while sexism is now, ostensibly, frowned upon, pop culture is slower than your Great-Uncle Geoffrey in accepting that a woman really shouldn't be called 'Toots' and slapped on something he calls 'the hiney'.

It's extraordinary how little some things have changed over the past thirty-five years since Faye Dunaway refused to stop working, thereby driving her exasperated lover away in the film *Network*. If Hollywood were to make a film of Hillary Clinton's recent few years, they would have Bill leave her during her presidential campaign because she loses sight of what really matters in life, i.e. him. She would then proceed to lose the election, move to the countryside in ignominy, get together with a hot plumber who lives down the road and rediscover the important things, like making apple sauce.

And so, with feminism somewhat stuck at this awkward halfway point, it is perhaps not surprising that the road to full-blooded feminism is paved with many perilous potholes that can cause even the most determined driver to derail.

These potholes have nothing to do with high heels and armpit hair – both of which any feminist is smart enough to do with as she sees fit – but are rather the ingrained habits and certain products that are the Trojan horses of antifeminism, things that only damage women's self-esteem and feminism in general, often in the guise of being part of a woman's culture. If I were a self-lobotomising women's magazine that tolerated stupid coinages like 'frenemies', then I'd say that that's what the following are. But I don't and so I'll simply say that if there were any justice in this cold, cruel world of ours, all of the following would be illegal.

1. Cure yourself of that nasty case of Self-Deprecating Tourettes

Here's a quick'n'easy cut-out'n'keep quiz for all the family (although don't cut it out until you read whatever's on the other side of the page. Or if you've borrowed this book from the library or a friend. Or are just reading it standing in the bookshop with no intention of actually paying for it, you cheap bastard):

If someone says, 'You look lovely in that dress', do you say:
a) 'Oh, yeah, well, the cut is amazing. You can't even tell I just put on half a stone. I'm amazed I can still fit in it, actually – God bless stretchy fabrics, eh?'
b) 'What, this piece of rubbish? I got it ten years ago from New Look.'
c) 'Thank you.'
d) 'Nowhere near as amazing as you look in that coat!'

An old friend has just sent you an email saying she heard about your recent promotion and is so happy for you. Do you
a) Write back: 'Ha, yeah, I think HR made a mistake and got the wrong [insert your name here]! I'm keeping schtoom, mind!'

b) Write back: 'Oh well, first one in ten years. It's not so much a promotion as a reward for longevity.'

c) Write back: 'Thank you!'

d) Not write back at all out of embarrassment. After all, what can you say that won't sound like bragging?

You bump into someone you haven't seen for a while. 'So what's new with you?' they ask. You say:

a) 'Oh, you know me, same ol', same ol', nothing to report. How about you?'

b) 'Well, Felix Cat Food has just added a new flavour – tuna and rice. As you can imagine, that was a BIG excitement in our household.'

c) 'I just got a promotion, actually. That's why I'm wearing this, my favourite dress, as I'm off to have a glass of champagne at the bar down the road to celebrate. Why don't you come?'

d) 'I'm getting over the flu, which is why I look even worse than usual.'

If you answered anything other than c) to any of the above then, well, I'm afraid I have bad news: you are suffering from Self-Deprecating Tourettes.

Now, now, don't worry, it's totally treatable. The important thing is that we caught it because while Self-Deprecating Tourettes isn't fatal, it can be very debilitating if left undetected. A little like chlamydia, but less fun to catch. It can afflict either gender but is far more common in women, so much so that it is not hyperbolic to refer to it as an epidemic. According to recent, highly scientific studies, 90 per cent of women suffer from it and of the remaining 10 per cent, 8 per cent were too busy putting themselves down for not knowing all the answers to the above quiz to be fully diagnosed, 1 per cent were too busy to take part and a mere 1 per cent remained healthy. For now. (Note: this problem is particularly common among British women and claims a relatively high proportion of British male sufferers too, because self-deprecation is pretty much part of the British accent. This does not make the disease any less damaging but rather exacerbates the problem by legitimising it and even, ridiculously, valuing it as a charming character trait.)

Quite why so many women are prone to this terrible illness is not definitively established but one theory does seem to be the most likely. Self-deprecation is often confused with modesty and modesty is pretty much the defining characteristic of femininity which itself is still widely seen as the most important quality to being a woman. Ergo, to be a woman is to be self-deprecating and, ultimately, self-defeating, a concept which is, for this woman to write, self-depressing.

Or it would be were it true, or even logical, and it is, in fact, demonstrably neither of these things.

Let's work backwards here. The idea that putting yourself down and saying that you're fat, boring and stupid makes one appear feminine relies on the assumption that the other person also converses in the parlance of self-deprecation and can translate accordingly. Otherwise, you're just saying that you're fat, boring and stupid and while femininity might be a subjective concept, I'm pretty sure no one considers fatness, dullness and stupidity as essential components of it. If the person does converse in that parlance, then they'll understand that you're actually praising yourself which is precisely what you're not supposed to be doing. Lose-lose!

Next, consider the mentality behind rejecting a compliment, a key sign that one suffers from Self-Deprecating Tourettes. After all, my God, to accept a compliment without the rebuffing shield of a self-deprecating deflection? Well, you're essentially saying that you agree with the praise which is a repulsive show of arrogance, right?

Well, there is, funnily enough, a whole gamut of expressions between arrogance and self-deprecation, and so just because one isn't being the latter does not mean one is necessarily the former.

Also, if all this is in aid of the misguided cause of femininity (itself a dubious and nebulous cause and concept), it achieves the opposite. It's not charming. In fact, it's rude and it's annoying. It's the verbal equivalent of throwing a present back in someone's face and telling them they're an idiot for having picked it out for you in the first place.

But all this is, ultimately, by the bye. The real peril of it is that Self-Deprecating Tourettes can, if allowed to fester, infect the sufferer's brain and soul.

As anyone who ever studied a modern language at school knows, there is no better way to learn things than by boring, monotonous repetition. Thus, to be constantly saying that you don't deserve that compliment, that you are an idiot, that your life is so inexpressibly boring that details of your day could cure insomnia, the person you are most likely to convince of the truth of this is you.

Moreover, self-deprecation is – as discussed – predicated on the idea that to believe in oneself is synonymous with laughable, sneer-worthy lordliness.

I have even seen extreme cases in which a young woman is terrified of flirting with a gentleman who has caught her eye because, in her disease-ridden mind, to flirt suggests that she believes there is a possibility that the gentleman might like her back, and this is an unforgivable, even laughable show of arrogance.

It is particularly sad to see even one's idols gripped by this terrible disease, women who cannot stop themselves from apologising for the success that they have worked so hard to achieve. Tina Fey is probably the most high-profile example of this and her 2011 memoir, *Bossypants*, manages to be both a funny and deeply dismaying unintentional casebook study of Self-Deprecating Tourettes, in which references to her alleged plainness, gaucheness and klutziness outnumber tales of her patently true success by about a gajillion to one. This is a terrible state of affairs because Tina is, quite frankly, awesome. Thus, her self-deprecation is not just wrong but illogical. In April 2011 David Remnick, editor of the *New Yorker* magazine, interviewed Fey at a Barnes and Noble bookstore in New York to help promote her book and at one point she started talking about the time she auditioned to be a writer and performer on *Saturday Night Live*. In the classic manner of someone in the throes of Self-Deprecating Tourettes, Fey started doing her schtick, saying what a disaster she had been, how she said all the wrong things at all the wrong times and so on. When Remnick pointed out that she had, in fact, got the job, Fey's downcast eyes and quick head twitch away from the audience suggested that she was currently suffering a small cerebral implosion, which is what happens when Self-Deprecating Tourettes is confronted with the strong antibiotic of truth. Tina! You're awesome! For heaven's sake, let yourself enjoy it, you deserve it!

In contrast, Fey's former comedy partner from *Saturday Night Live* and good friend, Amy Poehler, gave a similar talk at the *New Yorker* Festival just six months later in October 2011. Instead of putting herself down, Poehler talked – honestly, sweetly and most of all, hilariously – about how hard she had worked to achieve her professional success. There was no suggestion of flukiness, no insistence on her klutziness. When the interviewer, *New Yorker* staff writer Ariel Levy, asked how she made the extremely difficult move from scrabbling stand-up to *Saturday Night Live*, Poehler replied simply, and without any arrogance, that the *SNL* people had seen some of her stand-up, liked it and so they summoned her in. And that was that. What made it so particularly appealing was that it was clearly the truth: Poehler is a very good comedian, therefore she got the most sought-after job in American comedy circles. Such things do not happen to people who are 'disasters'. When Levy showed some clips of Poehler's work over the years, Poehler, far from shying away in horror, or making some tedious reference to her changing body shape, simply laughed with pleasure. This is because Poehler does not suffer from the same disease as Fey, convulsing into awkwardness when confronted with her own success. She knows that a woman can be funny without belittling herself. But she is almost alone in that knowledge.

And this just will not do. If being a feminist means believing in women's rights, you cannot be a feminist if you do not believe in the most important woman's rights – your own.

Furthermore, it is worth remembering that Self-Deprecating Tourettes can manifest itself in a myriad of ways. You don't need to say explicitly that your point of view should be dismissed because you're so silly/boring/worthless

– you can do it through implication, and a particularly popular way for many women to do that is to talk in a silly voice.

In the often prescient and shockingly underrated British female sketch show, *Smack the Pony*, one particularly good skit was about a woman who appeared to be physically incapable of not talking in a comedy accent.

'Why are you talking like that?' asked her friend.

'Tawkin' lahk wot?' replied the accent-addicted woman, in a voice that seemed to go from Brooklyn to Newcastle by way of Liverpool.

Silly Speak is the frequent recourse for awkward exchanges (hence the popularity of comedy accents when having to make an apology – 'Ahhhh'm soooooray …'). One also occasionally hears it from women who are actually making serious points about themselves or current events, but somewhere between their thinking of these points and the points emanating from their mouth they appear to lose their nerve and resort to comedy accents.

And it's understandable why. To talk in a silly accent or to converse or – another all too popular tic among adults old enough to know better – faux teenage-speak (an over-reliance on text message acronyms, exclamation marks, capital letters, abbreviations derived from social media sites and Valley Girl language) might seem like an appealingly jokey way in which to convey whatever point you're trying to make, a way of saying whatever you have to or want to say, but with distracting verbal jazz hands. But the truth is, it actually suggests that what you're saying, and you, shouldn't be taken seriously.

This is not to suggest that being funny precludes anyone from being taken seriously. Personally, I've always thought that comedy conveys serious points far better than po-faced solemnity. But comedy accents and teenage talk, first, are not funny and, second, are self-undermining which means that they are self-deprecating.

Don't be embarrassed about making a point, or even just making your voice heard. Do it, and do it in your own voice. As Madonna says in one of the better feminist philosophical treatises put forward in the past decade 'Do You Know What it Feels Like For a Girl?', 'When you're trying hard to be your best could you be a little less?' The answer is, no, you couldn't and shouldn't. Just keep being your best, and smile and say thank you. (And incidentally, for every ten times you say the word 'sorry' in a day, nine of them are not just unnecessary but inappropriate. Rectify accordingly.)

1. a) By all means ask men about their achievements but then tell them about yours, too: An addendum to Self-Deprecating Tourettes

There is a theory that men are threatened by high-achieving, confident women and that the best way to please one is simply to ask him about his achievements, nod encouragingly and never use the first person pronoun except when saying a phrase like, 'I don't understand, could you please explain that to me again, o smart, manly man you?'

This is undoubtedly true – of some men. The question is, why would you really want to hang around such a silly specimen for any length of time at all?

I'm going to say something quite maverick here so hold on to your fascinators: not all men are self-centred jerks beset by egos more fragile than a fourteenth-century porcelain collection. In fact, there are – it's true! – quite a few nice ones.* A good way of sorting the promising wheat from the time-wasting chaff is, when you meet them, to ask what they've been up to and what they do, and then wait to see if they reciprocate. And if they do, look to see if they then actually listen or if they stare over your head in the hope that a waitress from Hooters will appear in their line of vision. It's a fun party game!

1. b) Accept that you don't have to be liked by everyone – and that's OK

This is definitely part of the tendency behind Self-Deprecating Tourettes problem. All too many women feel that, in order to fulfil their feminine criteria, they must ensure they are liked by everyone, from the handyman who just ripped them off ('I'm so sorry to bother you but that pipe you just fixed yesterday which you charged me a grand for, well, I don't know if I've done something wrong but it's exploded. Oh no, I'm sure it's not your fault …') to the stranger who just jumped them in the bus queue. I have a friend who was so concerned about making her weed dealer like her she used to send birthday cards to his kids, much to his bemusement. Obviously, this is, to a certain degree, a nice instinct, wanting to be kind to people. But all too often it is a self-stifling one, something that is holding you back from

---

* This, incidentally, is an addendum to an addendum. True feminists do not make tired sweeping statements about men because feminists know that jokes like 'What do you call the useless bit of skin at the end of a penis?' are just as unacceptable as jokes like 'How many women does it take to screw in a lightbulb?' Some women might be tempted to think otherwise and see it as a form of revenge for the centuries of sexist jokes their gender has had to endure, but gender stereotyping is not a particularly helpful tactic in attempting to achieve gender equality.

standing up for yourself and avoiding confrontation, and it is a needlessly distracting concern. Be polite to people, sure, but stop trying to make everyone your friend. They won't be. And that's just fine.

2. Be kind to yourself
To be a feminist means to live up to one's full potential, personally, professionally, mentally, morally. But it is impossible to do this if you can barely stand up straight from beating yourself up all the time and hobbling your own strength. This is not meant literally (I hope), but rather refers to the bruises one suffers from self-hatred. 'How could I be so stupid?' KA-POW! 'I'm so hungry but carbs will make me fat so I won't eat the bread and I'll be tired and hungry all afternoon.' THUNK! 'Hmm, I wonder what's happening on the *Daily Mail* website.' BOOM!

Self-Deprecating Tourettes we already talked about but another element to it, one arguably more damaging than when the self-deprecation is merely outwardly to other people, is when it is expressed inwardly and you are horrid about yourself, to yourself. Never talk to yourself in a way that you wouldn't put up with from other people and – if that is an unhelpful analogy because you have let people say some horrid things to you – never talk to yourself in a way that someone who loves you very, very much would not allow. In other words, stop calling yourself stupid when you forget to buy washing-up liquid on your way home and stop calling yourself fat because your jeans are chafing a tad. It's just bad manners.

In a lovely article about eating on one's own by Daisy Garnett that ran in the *Observer* newspaper in 2010, Garnett wrote: 'Eating sensibly and well when alone is a mark of self-respect.' This is goddamn true. But it is also true that eating sensibly and well full-stop is a sign of self-respect. The causes of eating disorders are myriad and complicated but one element that unites them all is self-hatred. Only someone who has no respect for themselves whatsoever can so wholly ignore their body's normal and increasingly desperate physical needs.

It is impossible to live up to your full potential if you are eating in a way that deprives you of energy, whether it is eating too much or too little. It is also impossible to accomplish anything if you are mentally engaged pondering whether calories or carbs are more fattening. There is no such thing as a perfect body type or perfect diet, no matter what any magazine or breakfast TV show might tell you: the only real goal is to have the energy to do the things you want to do, and enjoy them. It takes a lot of energy, physical and mental, to be a plucky feminist so it is your responsibility, not just to yourself but feminism in general, to eat well. So every time you catch yourself starting to obsess about food and weight, go have a massage or – if there is a person in the near vicinity worthy of such a privilege – some sexy time. Your body does great things for you every day and it deserves to be treated nicely.

3. Never be afraid of getting into an argument about abortion

Look, there's nothing to be frightened of here. Yes, abortion remains, 40 years after Roe v Wade, a deeply fraught issue, more so in America (where I'm from) than in the UK (where I live), and that is just one of the reasons why I, personally, find living in the UK a far more pleasant experience. I can only take listening to ignorant and opportunistic politicians talk about what a woman is allowed to do with her body for their own political gain for so long. And yes, some of those anti-choice people do look and sound pretty scary and they are fond of using impassioned, even gruesome arguments.

But this isn't complicated. It doesn't even have to be emotional. It simply comes down to the following question: whose needs and emotions are more important – those of the pregnant woman or those of the foetus inside her? That's it. The grown-up who actually exists as a human, or the bunch of cells inside her that do not.

To be anti-choice is to be anti-women. It is to see women as baby-carriers, not human beings. No woman should have to justify why she wants an abortion (which is why rape and incest exceptions in the US regarding tax payer assisted abortions are, in fact, red herrings. As Irin Carmon wrote, this idea suggests some 'abortions are worthier than others … either you believe a woman has the right to decide not to be pregnant anymore, or you think you should get a say in her decision'*). An abortion is not a pleasant procedure but its existence is inevitable and necessary and even if it's made illegal women will still find ways to have it, just in less safe ways.

So stand up for women and stand up yourself: if you believe that it is your body, your life, fight this fight.

4. Do not get distracted by phoney women vs women fights

Whether it really is the world's most cherished wish that all women would spend every hour of every day mud wrestling one another is something I do not know for certain. What I

---

* 'Rape exceptions aren't legitimate', Irin Carmon, *Salon*, 20 August 2012.

do know is that the media rub their sweaty thighs at the prospect of reducing something – anything – down to a possibly non-existent fight between at least two women or, as it is commonly but offensively called, 'a catfight', a term that shall ne'er be uttered by me again.

The classic example from the celebrity world was Jennifer Aniston vs Angelina Jolie, with veritable landfills of celebrity magazines and tabloid journalism detailing the terrible 'rivalry' between Jolie and Aniston, as though they were two scrapping toddlers and Brad Pitt was the grinning, hapless teddy bear who would helplessly go home with whomever picked him up. Rare, however, was the acknowledgement that Aniston's beef might have been more with Pitt, the husband who let her down, than the woman with whom he was now living. But then, you can't blame Brad, right? He's just a man, a giant, silly, brainless loin, helpless to his desires, whereas Jolie, as a woman, should have known better than to tempt him with her black magic ways.

Such nonsense is not restricted to the celebrity arena by any means. An article recently appeared in the US magazine the *Atlantic*, in which Anne-Marie Slaughter, the former Director of Policy for the US State Department, argued, in a thoughtful and measured piece, that women can't have it all – not now, anyway. Now, this question is, in itself, very interesting, pointing to, as it does, a lack of true gender equality in many relationships, the changes motherhood imposes on many women's mental and emotional priorities, the shocking lack of assistance from many employers when it comes to accommodating female employees' child-related responsibilities, the nightmarish difficulties of childcare arrangements and the sense of futility many women feel when faced with these cold realities. It also acts as a reminder that even those barriers are gifted to the fortunate few as lower income women don't even get the privilege of asking themselves the question if they can have it all because, when it comes to childcare and work, their choices are even more limited.

Sadly, such discussions were not the general response to this piece. Rather, it was spun as an argument between Slaughter and Facebook executive Sheryl Sandberg, who Slaughter referenced in her piece as being another woman who has talked about how women can 'have it all'. The obvious answer to this popular question now seemed, 'Well, probably not, but who can tell when the media are more interested in cooking up phoney lady fights than actually covering the issue?'

As most women know, different lives work for different women, and every woman's circumstance is different. The world is very imperfect and there is no single solution for women today, just as one woman's situation probably does not reflect that of women in general and so disagreements between women about how they live their lives do not signify some great inter-gender conflict. Women, contrary to the media's apparent belief, are not one homogenous whole (this is something politicians all too often forget when they use the term 'policies for women' to mean 'policies for parenthood': not only are not all women parents but not all parents are women). These phoney women versus women fights are mere mosquitoes, buzzing about and distracting people who should know better from far more important issues – indeed, the issues that the women were actually talking about before the media pushed them into the wrestling ring and begged them to fight. Let others be dazzled by such nonsense. As a feminist, you know better.

5. Have a very stern word with anyone who judges women more harshly than they judge men, even – especially! – if they don't realise they're doing it

Now, you could, I suppose, claim this is actually a feminist tendency: by judging other women more harshly than you judge men you are proving that you expect more of them, whereas men are just foolish little numbskulls, so gullible and easily pleased. But in order to maintain this argument you have to be of a similar mindset to the one that is able to claim that stripping is actually an empowering feminist activity without giving yourself an aneurysm. Women who can hear what they're saying as they speak are, in my experience, rarely able to do this. And also, taking a view of the genders that appears to be based on the laziest, most cliché-ridden of TV sitcoms – he's a hapless schlub! She's his smart but beleaguered wife! – is unlikely to provide much in the way of instructional value.

It would be very easy to point to multiple examples of women being crueller to one another than they are to men simply by flicking through any British newspaper in which, all too often on certain right-wing papers, the high-profile female columnists are used as Trojan horses in which to smuggle in the worst examples of misogyny. I could, for example, talk about the female columnist who wailed about the damage inflicted on her corneas by the photos of an unacceptably curvaceous eighteen-year-old Princess Beatrice in a bikini. Or the writer who sneered, with classic social snobbery, at Pippa Middleton's 'characteristic fake tan', her 'passably attractive looks' and her attendance at a 'second-tier university' while tutting at her for 'loving the limelight'*

---

* 'Cat Who Got the Cream!', Catherine Ostler, *Daily Mail*, 28 April 2011.

(apparently the writer was unaware that she was, in fact, writing an article that provides this aforementioned and very NQOCD 'limelight'). Similarly, I could point out that it was only female journalists who chastised French politician Rachida Dati for returning to work four days after giving birth, as though it was the business of these self-appointed protectors of proper maternal conduct to comment on how another woman runs her own life.

But to be honest, using the behaviour of the British media as an illustration of gender relations is like pointing to Fred West as proof that the familial unit is breaking down. So instead, let's keep this simple, straight and realistic and list what women should not do to other women.

Don't, when reading a story about a marital breakdown, instantly blame the mistress while letting the husband off scot-free (a good exercise to help you accustom yourself to this seemingly novel idea is to repeat the following and apparently little known mantra in front of a mirror every morning: 'It was Brad who made and broke the commitment to Jen, not Angelina. It was Brad who made and broke the commitment to Jen, not Angelina').

Do not stay silent if anyone ever suggests – obliquely or otherwise – that the looks or behaviour of the victim of sexual harassment or assault are in any way to blame for the trauma inflicted, or that the victim's reaction proves that she is weak and she really just needs to man up, so to speak. Remind this person that rape is not an expression of unleashed male desire. It is an extreme expression of sadism, bullying and/or mental illness and can happen to anyone, even – contrary to what Hollywood seems to believe – people who are not young, female and blonde, because rape is not a compliment, doled out only to the beautiful or alluring. To suggest anything otherwise is not only a disgusting slur on the victim but pretty insulting to men in general as it suggests that they are all barely contained gormless rapists.

Never cast judgement on another woman's weight, parenting skills, marriage or general lifestyle, unless you do it to men too. But really, don't do it to either gender. It's just ugly.

Don't assume that a woman who writes an emotional memoir is a self-indulgent narcissist, whereas a man who does the same is brave and something described as 'searing'.

Should you overhear anyone doing any of the above, it is your feminist responsibility to give them a very cross wag of your finger.

6. Be a feminist, not a faux feminist

When women of Gaga's mindset claim not to be feminists, they often explain this by saying that they don't want special treatment or to be defined by their gender ('I'm not a feminist. I consider my position in the business world not as a woman but as a person, and I don't think, "Did that happen because I'm a woman?"').* They always say this with a snap of pride in their voice, as though they are making not just the definitive, argument-closing point, but one that has not been said a kajillion times before, which does raise some questions about whether they are really as well read as they invariably claim to be, but that's a different issue. What they don't quite seem to get, though, is that is precisely the point of feminism: not to be limited or defined by one's gender.

For a woman to say that she doesn't call herself a feminist is like a black person announcing he's racist. And yet, it's

---

* Entrepreneur Deborah Meaden, *Guardian*, 9 September 2009.

astonishing how often one comes across interviews with female celebrities who refuse to define themselves as feminists. Despite playing in a film one of the most famous feminists of all time, Gloria Steinem, Sarah Jessica Parker insists, 'I'm not a feminist, I'm a humanist.' Similarly, Gwyneth Paltrow recounted in one interview about how she recently gave advice to a friend in a new relationship: 'I said this may not be feminist, but you have to compromise … Gloria Steinem may string me up by my toes.' Fortunately for Paltrow and her toes it is unlikely Steinem would do any such thing because, contrary to what Paltrow seems to believe, feminism is not about selfishness, lack of compromise, hating men, special treatment or tokenism: it's about equality. Nor does it mean a woman should wear boiler suits and obliterate all traces of her natural femaleness, but rather that she should expect to be seen as the strong, intelligent and capable person that she is, with a voice worth listening to and a brain deserving of respect. If you ever meet a woman – or anyone, for that matter – who says they're not a feminist, ask them if they believe women are human beings who deserve all the same opportunities as other human beings. Because, honestly, that's all it is. Not favouritism – equality. You don't need to have a vagina to be a feminist, although if you do have one and are not a feminist, you don't deserve the privilege of possessing that vagina.

Maybe it's because I have a name that makes me sound less like a person and more like an investment bank but I have always been interested in the subject of nomenclature and, specifically, how, when poorly executed, it can lead to wrong impressions.

Feminism can be a somewhat misleading term, like 'global warming'. 'Global warming' encourages climate change deniers and anyone else whose comprehension of science is less than that of a fifteen-year-old to snicker triumphantly every time a snowflake falls, which they probably burn on a phosphate pyre in celebration.

Feminism's name is to gender equality what global warming is to climate change: the same idea but with a name that can cause some confusions and make it an unnecessary target for the dull-witted sceptics. Just as 'global warming' doesn't mean that the world is actually heating up but rather is being inexorably altered, feminism doesn't mean women should take precedence over men but rather that they are equal.

To take a woman's side automatically because she is a woman is not real feminism – that is faux feminism and faux feminism is as toxic to the cause as subtle misogyny because both make a mockery out of the real ambition here and obscure it; the difference is that faux feminism doesn't even know it is doing it.

Thus for Harriet Harman to claim that Lehman Brothers would not have collapsed had women been in charge, or for Lynne Featherstone – the Equalities Minister, for heaven's sake! – to say that 'you get terrible decisions' when men are in charge is as reductive as the late Christopher Hitchens's too-often repeated comment about women not having a sense of humour. All men may have penises, but not all men are the same. You have more to offer than your gender and don't want to be reduced to it. Don't do it to others, either.

Complications come in with the question of whether women need the lifting hand of positive discrimination quotas even to get to the level of equality. There are, unquestionably, still some rather anti-female playing fields out there that need levelling, circumstances in which women remain hobbled by everything from difficulties with childcare to straight-out chauvinism and both of these factors lead to a distinct under-representation of women in various industries. My personal feeling is that instead of having all-female book prizes, say, practical long-term solutions might be more effective, such as lobbying for all places of employment to offer free childcare facilities and tackling the actual issues that hold women back. But I am an idealist.

6. a) Don't define yourself by your age or your size

Let's all do an exercise. Write a list of the top five characteristics that you think define you. 'Smart', perhaps? 'Likes bungee jumping', maybe? 'Big fan of Carole King'? Anything really. Now, look over that list. Is there anywhere a reference to your size or your age? There is? OK, we're going to have to have a talk. Make yourself comfortable.

Your body is not you. It is just your body, and it should no more dictate your personality than an aeroplane determines the quality of your holiday: it is merely a vessel that gets you from A to B. It is very easy to forget this in a world where one's body is often presented as one's personal achievement, an outward manifestation of one's inner qualities and, therefore, proof of what one is worth. It is a sad state of affairs when a mentality that should be limited to cheesy advertisements for exercise equipment becomes a general given, but that does not mean you have to accept it and, as a feminist, you definitely should not. Feminists are too smart for this self-reductive nonsense.

This idea that physicality does not, in fact, dictate personality might surprise anyone who gleans their understanding of humanity from films or TV shows where it is the law for any woman who is overweight to be sassy and loud or, alternatively, miserable and quiet but finds redemption either by losing weight and/or discovering she has an amazing singing voice. And if you have the misfortune to be fat in a children's book, particularly one written by Roald Dahl, then I'm afraid I have some bad news for you: you are spoilt, stupid and, most likely, evil.

Because of this message that a woman's appearance determines not just her personality but the quality of her life, it is very easy to be persuaded that if you have a physical quality that is overvalued by the gym advert of a world we now live in, you should then draw attention to it, repeatedly. Tell-tale signs that a woman has fallen victim to this mentality are if she says versions of the following remarks:

'Oh, you're so lucky you can wear bracelets. My wrists are so tiny they always just fall right off me!'

'I ran three miles today and because I'm so ickle that was like six miles for me!'

'Every time I go to America, I get asked for my ID all the time. I guess it's because I look so young!'

'I love going to Asia because the clothes there are so small. It's the only place I can buy jeans that fit properly!'

There is nothing wrong – in fact, there is everything good – about having a sense of pride in yourself. But this is not pride – it's tragic and any use of the word 'ickle' makes it even more unbearable.

True, I don't actually know you personally but I feel very secure in saying that you have plenty of other qualities that are far more interesting and commendable than your size and your youth, both of which, incidentally, are temporal. I say that not out of a desire to be mean, but a desire to help because it will be all the more difficult for you when they change if you persuaded yourself early on that they were what define you. Overvaluing youth and slimness has only two possible end results: miserable self-loathing, or miserable self-loathing coupled with an addiction to plastic surgery. Yes, fashion fetishises youth and slimness, but this does not mean you have to go along with that fetishisation. If anything, it means precisely the opposite: after all, why trust an industry that every four years promotes dropped-crotch trousers?

So as well as not talking about how you're so tiny you have to buy your clothes in Baby Gap, don't, if you are over the age of eighteen, refer to yourself as a 'girl' or your friends, if they are over eighteen, as 'the girls'. You are a woman and a lady and so are they. And you know what? That's just brilliant.

6. b) And also, don't lose your individuality in a relationship or define yourself by it

There is an old cliché that says that men define themselves by professional success and women define themselves by their love life. Personally, I'm suspicious of any statement that suggests 50 per cent of the human race all think the same way because they have similar genitals but this statement has a crumb of truth to it, albeit not in the way it suggests. It is not that every single woman sees marriage and motherhood as the only routes to self-validation; rather, that is how they are valued in the media and pop culture. Men, while not immune to this, certainly suffer from this to a much, much lesser extent. Personally, I judge myself by whether I can still spell 'Ralph Macchio' without having to Google it but, hey, to each their own.

It is your duty as a modern feminist to disprove this tedious cliché by not falling victim to it yourself. Personally, I'm a big advocate for supporting yourself financially for as long as possible, simply because I think it's a boon to one's self-respect and sense of individuality. Even if your partner earns more and likes to 'spoil' you, for your own personal wellbeing it is healthy to know you can look after yourself at least as well as he can. So learn how to do your taxes, sort out your mortgage and pay your way in life in general. Claiming to be a 'ditz with money' is, quite simply, not an acceptable excuse.

Similarly, when asked how you're doing, don't reply with a long discussion about how your husband, boyfriend or children are – answer about yourself. When asked for your opinions on matters political, televisual or just general, don't give your partner's opinions instead of your own. Even if you now think of yourself as part of a unit, your friends still see and love you as an individual. Unless you are at an event specifically for your husband or children, don't introduce yourself as someone's 'wife' or 'mummy', and do not use that description in your Facebook and Twitter biography. It is lovely that you are so happy in your matrimonial or maternal role but that is a happiness that is most valued within the family unit. Outside it, you are an individual, and this is for your own sake as much as anyone else's: as nice as it is to be in a happy relationship, it is not healthy to define yourself solely by it. You are still a '*tu*' as well as a '*vous*' and that's fabulous.

7. Stand your ground against Bully Mothers

My lovely, newly babied up friends have given me many insights into motherhood previously unappreciated by me. They have taught me, for example, how incredibly hard and all encompassing it is, something I never appreciated at all, really, with my own mother. They have also taught me how shockingly expensive prams are, costing my friends more than, in some cases, a second-hand car.

But even more disturbing than that, they have taught me, in whispered, horror struck tones, about the Bully Mother, a heretofore unknown to me species who roams the playgroups, NCT groups and school gates of our land.

Bully Mothers are women who find some form of self-vindication in making other women – mothers and non-mothers – doubt their choices because their choices happen to be different from those of the Bully Mothers. Common tender points that the Bully Mothers aim for are at what age a woman has children, whether she has pain-relieving drugs, whether she has the baby at home or in a hospital, whether she breast-feeds the baby and for how long, whether she goes back to work and when, when she puts the baby down for school and which one, etc., etc. ad fricking nauseam. Sometimes such claims are not even directed specifically at one woman but rather at all women in general who dared to have different approaches to motherhood from those of the Bully Mother. In June 2012 Cherie Booth felt compelled to sneer about a nebulous demographic called 'yummy mummies' at an event for 'Most Powerful Women', an occasion that should, one might have thought, been about celebrating women as opposed to deriding them: 'You hear these yummy mummies talk about being the best possible mother and they put all their effort into their children. I also want to be the best possible mother, but I know that my job as a mother includes bringing my children up so actually they can live without me,' Booth declared, apparently in the belief that the way to argue against those with a didactic mindset about motherhood is to be equally and intractably didactic oneself.

There is something impressive about anyone who is so convinced of their own rectitude, plagued by not a fleeting glimpse of self-doubt, unconcerned about their possibly negative impact on others. But that is not quite what is going on here. In some instances, the Bully Mother is an agent planted by advocates of the Overpopulation Society who believe that too many people have too many children and the fake Bully Mother's job is to roam the earth and put women off from having children out of fear they will turn into her as soon as the epidural wears off. Others are a victim of a secret plot cooked up by the *Daily Mail* in which some women had their brains removed and replaced by a chip that made them parrot the editorial practices of that tabloid.

Finally, and most commonly, others are blocking out the inner screeches of insecurity that echo in their own brains by talking incessantly about how infallible they are, and how flawed everyone else is. But remember this: any woman who finds self-validation by boasting about the method of childbirth she chose and tutting at the one you opt for is a woman who should be pitied because she clearly doesn't think her life has much else to offer.

There is no one child-rearing practice that will guarantee a happy, healthy, well-adjusted child. Yet one thing that won't make anyone feel happy and well-adjusted is lots of Bully Mothers stomping around, judging other women's mothering practices. So stand up to the Bully Mother.

Of course, this is not simple; she tends to be quite scary and it is easy to believe that, with her ringing tone of certainty, she may be right. It is particularly difficult when you are a mother yourself and worn down with fatigue and general panic that you are doing something so terrible that your child will grow up to be the next Jeffrey Dahmer, chopping up male prostitutes and keeping their limbs in the freezer. This is why Bully Mothers are so effective: they have a very vulnerable target base.

But these people know nothing. Repeat, nothing. You know yourself and your child better than they do. Trust yourself. Yet it can be hard to get these Bully Mothers to hush up, leave you alone and to stop trying to make other women feel bad about themselves. Here are some sample responses that you can make to the Bully Mothers to accomplish just that:

'Huh. Could you recommend an ear specialist to me? Because, you see, I didn't actually hear myself asking your opinion on when you think I should have a baby and, seeing as you have all the right answers, of course, I'm sure any doctor I found would be nowhere near as good as the one you go to.'

'That's so interesting that you think I'm traumatising my child by not breast-feeding him. Seeing as you're so concerned for his welfare, obviously you'll do it for me. Here you go – he gets particularly hungry at about 3 a.m.'

'Out of curiosity, in which child-rearing book did you read that the best kind of mother is an insecure one? Well, whatever, thank you for helping me become that mother! Now, what do you think your address will be in, oh, sixteen years? I'll need it to send my child's future therapy bills to you, of course.'

7. a) And don't pay any attention to their single lady equivalents

There is a popular genre of journalism, beloved by both US and UK publications, which I like to call the Ghosts of Female Youths Past. These articles nearly always adhere to the following formula: they are usually first person; they are illustrated with a photo of the female writer, arms crossed with a look of wistfulness undercut with a sense of betrayal; they open with a description of the thirty- or forty-something woman's sad, regret-filled single life; they move swiftly into a diatribe about the failures and dangers of feminism that have led them to this sad place, followed by cod anthropological claims that have led to the State of Women Now; they then return to the first person with the writer expressing regrets about the men she turned down in her youth because she wanted an unspecified 'More'; they conclude with a sense of self-flagellation dressed up as 'honesty' about feminism.

The American magazine the *Atlantic* is very fond of publishing such pieces* as is, unsurprisingly, the *Daily Mail*,*2

---

* 'Marry Him', Lori Gottlieb, *Atlantic*, 2008; 'All the Single Ladies', Kate Bolick, *Atlantic*, 2011.

*2 'Too Laid Back, Too Sexy, Too Independent: why some women just AREN'T wife material', Frances Childs, *Daily Mail*, 21 November 2011; 'Amanda Platell on Yearning for Motherhood', Amanda Platell, *Daily Mail*, 13 December 2011.

proving that the most unlikely of publications can unite in the Venn diagram of Making Women Feel Bad for Believing in Feminism, publishing articles that play on women's fears as nervily as the Bully Mother herself.

Of course, one feels terribly sorry for the writers of these pieces if they are so disappointed in the current state of their lives. It is, unquestionably, a difficult thing to accept that your life is not going to adhere to the expectations you had for it and maybe certain things that you'd always taken for granted aren't going to happen, or at least not when you expected them to do so.

However, universalising one's own unhappiness into being a comment on Women Today is not helpful or even legitimate. Sure, one's elders are free to pass on lessons but one's elders' issues are not, contrary to what the elder may think, necessarily a comment on feminism.

Life doesn't always work out as one expected. That is an occasionally jarring truth. But here's another truth: women are individuals, and not all experiences that happen to one woman reflect the condition of all women. Women have more choices now – which is a good thing – and, yes, that may then disrupt the conventional chronology of one's life. Not everyone's life, mind: one's life. Whether having those choices is, in itself, a bad thing is an idea with which I would quibble most roundly.

So in short, to paraphrase the Great and Glorious Wizard of Oz, pay no attention to the Ghosts of Female Youths Past behind the bylines in your magazine and newspaper. You are your own individual person and you have your own expectations about your life and will have your own individual life experiences. As a feminist, it is your job to carve your own path and not to allow your hopes and ambitions to be cowed and shrunken by doomsayers who are curdled with regrets about their own lives. You know yourself better than they do. And honestly, who would you trust more: someone who poses in a national publication with the requisite wistful/betrayed expression, or your own good self? Case, rested, etc.

8. Don't be a passive consumer of the media

I'm going to let you in on a secret, a revelation, even, one culled from my decade of working at the beating heart of the British media: everything a newspaper does, it does to get more readers.

It would be nice to think that newspapers – particularly the more rabidly fanatical and misogynistic newspapers – say the things they say and do the things they do in order to pursue some strange political agenda. But the simple if somewhat terrifying truth is that they do those things because THEY THINK READERS WANT THEM TO (and even more terrifyingly, judging from their relatively high circulation figures apparently quite a few do). They are not trying to change the world, they are trying to sell newspapers and make money.

This is particularly true as we are all at some weird twilight era of what is already, heartbreakingly, being called 'old media', when the newspaper will be seen as much of an unimaginable anachronism as an un-Botoxed actress.

So if a newspaper is doing something that offends your feminist principles, you are now in a particularly strong position to rectify this. Don't just stand on the sidelines complaining about how mean the newspapers are about women. In short, what I'm saying is, the way to read a newspaper like a feminist is to complain. A lot.

Of course, sometimes it's hard to see the wood for the trees, particularly when the trees have lost their lives so needlessly in order to host pictures of Page 3 girls.

And so, to help get you started, here are some things you might consider complaining about to a newspaper: when a woman is interviewed, her age and marital status are mentioned in the first paragraph whereas when a man is interviewed, his aren't until, at the earliest, the fifth paragraph, if at all; any articles that focus on a woman's weight, looks, marriage or maternal practices; the use of, say, a photo of Angelina Jolie to illustrate a news story about the Sudan (she went there once? Maybe?); a notable over-fondness for using the byline photos of the young female journalists but a definite lack of ones of their female colleagues who happened to have been born thirty years earlier; any articles that work under the assumption that if a woman hasn't married or had children she is somehow a bit weird or, at the very least, tragic.

Effective ways of complaining include bellowing about them – with cold, hard, non-hysterical reason, of course – on social media sites, such as Facebook, Twitter (although don't link to the article itself as that will only give the website more hits which defeats the purpose). Or you could find out the editor's email address (never very difficult – they're often on the articles on the internet), and that of the letters page. Then, write a calm and short email stating precisely what your objection is and why. Do not lean on THE CAPS LOCK KEY as you write, rip the exclamation button off your keyboard if you find it impossible to resist that siren call under emotional times, and do not bring in any objections you might also have to the paper's stance on the war and the fact there are never any good recipes in the magazine. Your letter needs to shame the journalist and editor with its focus, intelligence and irrefutable rightness. Its feminism, in other words.

9. Accept that the things you feel and/or do occasionally that you worry aren't feminist are, in fact, unfeminist

Wanting to be with someone and have a family is not unfeminist. What is unfeminist is believing that the only truly satisfying life for a woman to have is to be married and have children and to try to convince other women of your viewpoint. But if being without a partner in your life makes you feel lonely because you genuinely want to be with someone as opposed to thinking you should because that is the accepted norm, then there is nothing treacherous about that.

Similarly, a woman who enjoys fashion is not any less of a feminist than a man who is interested in cars is misogynistic. Unfortunately, both of these subjects get covered by magazines and TV shows in a manner that does cause some problems. Car aficionados, for example, must suffer the indignity of being associated with racist jokes and terrible metaphors thanks to *Top Gear*, while fashion fans are forced to squint past the anorexia, the celebrities, the shameless adoration of wealth and the frankly atrocious gush that fill most fashion magazines in order to see the clothes that they love.

It is hard to see how spending money you earn on clothes that you like and make you feel good about yourself is unfeminist. Clothes are a particularly enjoyable form of self-expression available more to women than to men. Take advantage of this. Men have to channel their longing for such fun into such sad and limiting channels as cufflinks and watches out of fear that anything more adventurous than a T-shirt and jeans will result in people questioning their sexuality.

This is why so many men often make fun of women's fashion and, particularly, women who enjoy fashion: because they're jealous. There is absolutely no intellectual difference between enjoying fashion and enjoying, say, sport, other than that the dress you buy from a fashion designer will last a lot longer than a ticket to a football game.

Moreover, some men get cross about fashion because, as they repeatedly claim, fashion isn't sexy: the models are too skinny, the clothes are often weird and, goddamnit, where are the boobs? In other words, they feel that their desires are being ignored, poor babies.

But what they don't understand is that fashion isn't about looking sexy, it's about looking different, and that's why it's so awesome. Or rather, it should be.

Unfortunately, much of the coverage of fashion does not help you in arguing that fashion is a feminist pursuit because it focuses on how it can make you look slimmer, sexier, most of all, like everybody else for the next six months. This season green is de rigueur, you know.

None of this is feminist because, of course, all of it is nonsense. Wear what you like because it's you who will be looking back at your outfit from the mirror, not Anna Wintour. And if Wintour does see your daringly not-on-trend outfit, she will doubtless applaud your courage and originality. Maybe.

And to be honest, who cares? You are a feminist and you will wear purple even when everyone else is wearing green. It's what your sisters fought for.

Speaking of purple and green and all shades of the rainbow, let's talk about make-up and beauty in general. Oh where, asks Elizabeth Bennet in the middle of *Pride and Prejudice*, does discretion end and avarice begin? And where, I ask myself at the end of this book, does taking pleasure in one's appearance end and kowtowing to some evil commercialised and masochistic ideal begin?

Lizzy Bennet eventually masters the issue of avarice and discretion, or at least masters it enough to marry her grumpy but wealthy neighbour which, in the world of marriage plot novels, is the important issue anyway.

The question about whether following various beauty regimes is a betrayal of one's feminist principles is, however, as yet unresolved and the resolution does not guarantee marriage to Mr Darcy (thank the Lord – honestly, of all the Austen heroes, sour-faced Fitzwilliam Darcy remains the pin-up? Captain Wentworth any day of the week for me and Sundays, too). Various writers have expended an extraordinary amount of energy debating this subject, energy that occasionally feels very misdirected.

'You work on your appearance in order to create a marketable image that can be bought and sold. Women are willingly turning themselves into commodities we can trade for our own and others' gain,'* wrote one journalist,

---

* 'Beauty Regime Change: the lost art of not looking good', Charlotte Raven, *Guardian*, 24 March 2012.

making a fairly hefty, presumptuous and common gender generalisation. 'Today, I pledge I will go and pick up my daughter without changing out of my husband's cat-hair-covered fleece, proud to be seen as someone with something better to do than de-lint,' she continued, thus getting right to the nub of the real problem with these kinds of articles. Judging women by their appearance is precisely the opposite of one of feminism's most central tenets and so to argue that to look dishevelled is the only acceptably feminist look is just as shallow and judgemental as to insist that feminine beauty is dependent on rouged cheeks and pinked lips.

A common plaint in every article arguing against make-up and beauty regimes (and fashion, come to that) is that they are so evil and addictive that poor little women become helpless to the compulsion. 'Looking good,' according to the aforementioned article, 'is a tedious full-time job,' while Julie Burchill, never one to let subtleties or facts trip her up on the road to a good rant, describes a strange world in which a woman is expected to 'spend three-quarters of my time and money turning myself into a hairless, poreless living doll'.* Maybe some women are indeed so in thrall to their own neuroses and believe everything they read in the *Sunday Times Style* magazine to the letter so that they structure their lives around eyebrow threading appointments and facials, but to claim that all do drips heavily of condescension and tips swiftly over into

---

* 'Spare me from the Whining Women who are Giving Feminism a Bad Name', Julie Burchill, *Observer*, 29 January 2012.

misogyny.* It is at least partly because of limiting nonsense like this that many young women today hesitate before describing themselves as feminists: because they think feminism is about self-imposed limitations, female in-fighting, joylessness and homogeneity when it is, of course, about precisely the opposite.

There are many, many things one can and should object to about the beauty industry: the creepy plastic surgery, the hair extensions that rip out pieces of one's scalp, the nonsensical yet ubiquitous term 'anti-ageing'. Truly, there is much about today's beauty industry that makes eighteenth-century treatments such as rib-breaking corsets and lead-poisoning face powder look like pampering.

---

* Further examples of misogynistic talk being used under the pretence of making a feminist argument against the beauty industry include 'women [who have beauty treatments] are, perhaps, unloved. But rather than admit that they may be unloved because they are unlovable – dull, clingy, humourless – they presume one more treatment will put it right …
Sex-starved saddo[s] who feel a bit hollow and have to pay to be touched' ('A Suitable Case for Treatment', *Guardian*, 23 February 2008); 'So who sets these ever-climbing standards of poreless, hairless, paranoid hygiene? It's women rather than men; women who have very little successful sex, perhaps, and seek to be touched with tenderness to the tragic extent they are prepared to pay for it' ('Why I Loathe the Creepy Cult of Pampering', *Daily Mail*, 9 February 2012); 'The spa culture is the foremost marketplace where the twin maladies of modern women – narcissism and self-loathing – meet up and conspire to rob them of their hard-earned cash, all the time pumping out the mantra that every woman is, or can be, beautiful … A plain woman is still plain after a week at Champney's. Let's face it, we are not Italy or Sweden; "beautiful" is not the default setting for the British female (or male). And no amount of time and money is going to turn a sow's ear into a silk purse, no matter how many seaweed wraps the poor fool shells out for' ('Face it, Ladies, Most of Us Will NEVER Be Pretty!', *Daily Mail*, 11 August 2011). As you have perhaps guessed from the repetition in arguments and homogeneity of tone, all the above examples were penned by one Julie Burchill.

But make-up and beauty treatments of the kind Burchill so objects to (massages, facials, pedicures, etc.) are not among those things. They are among the increasingly rare offerings by the beauty industry that are, in fact, just for the women themselves as opposed to some imagined gaze of others.

When a woman puts on make-up, she is not going to look younger; she is creating her version of glamour and while one can argue that this proves she is kowtowing to some kind of masochistic ideal, it is surely far more offensive to assume that women can't tell the difference on their own between being enslaved by western beauty ideals and enjoying themselves.

Burchill's characteristically measured response disputes that – "'I'm doing it for me, not for men" – oh, give it a rest, you lying cow!'* – but, as she herself says, 'Straight men couldn't care less [about women's beauty regimes] – they generally just want women to have a wash, bring beer, show up and strip off.'*2 Whether this equally reductive gender stereotype is any more accurate than the ones she makes about women is another issue; the point is, contrary to what Burchill seems to believe, she is not the only woman out there who knows that men don't give a damn if a woman has moisturised skin or polished nails. However, what other women do know that she apparently does not is that not everything a woman does is for the benefit of men.*3

---

* 'Spare me from the Whining Women who are Giving Feminism a Bad Name', op. cit.

*2 Ibid.

*3 Burchill seems to find this a terrible thing, asking, 'When did women whose looks are not their living start conducting themselves like simpering inmates of an Ottoman empire seraglio?' (ibid.) It's an odd argument, suggesting that women of normal looks don't deserve to treat themselves and feel good about themselves. Clearly a bizarre point of view so let's not waste any more of this footnote upon it.

Journalists have a most unfortunate tendency to assume that members of the public are a great deal stupider than themselves and nowhere is this tendency more pronounced than in articles by female journalists raging against the tyranny of the beauty industry for women.

Feminism gives women choice and freedom and while this can be and sometimes is turned in on itself to be used against women ('Women! You have the freedom to dress as Playboy bunnies! It's a feminist thing!'), here is a quick checklist to ascertain if something is not feminist:

1. Does it hurt women?
2. Does it reduce women to a stereotype and/or her sexuality?
3. Does it encourage women to damage themselves physically?
4. Does it stop women from living their lives to the fullest of their capabilities?
5. Does it suggest that only a very particular kind of woman (under thirty/thin/a mother) is an acceptable woman?

Seeing as the answer to all the above in regard to make-up and non-surgical beauty treatments is no, they've got a free feminist pass. So if eye shadow and body scrubs are what float your boat, float away.

10. Understand what feminism actually is, and how it involves Glamorgan

Feminism is about enabling women to live the kind of lives that they want to live, whether that is living on their own on the top of Mount Rushmore in a crevice on Abraham Lincoln's head; in a small house in the suburbs of Glamorgan with five kids and a husband called Kevin; or wearing a burlap skirt or a couture gown by Chanel; as made up as Marilyn Manson or as barefaced as the day you were born. It's about freedom, individuality and being allowed to enjoy yourself and not shaping yourself to a pre-existing stereotype or allowing your glorious personality and your fabulous opinions to be overshadowed by clichés or insecurities but rather to live as the individual you are. It is about being kind and supportive of other women, not just because they are women but because you are a kind and supportive person and you know that helping other people – male or female – is much more conducive to a better life for yourself and better world in general than sniping and backbiting. It is allowing you to live, to quote – bringing us back to where we started – the lovely if, admittedly, not obviously feminist film, *The Princess Bride*, as you wish.

When to listen to your friends, and when not to

LISTEN

1. 'Never mind what he's thinking, what do you actually want?'
2. 'Do not send that email.'
3. 'I'm really not sure if your mother is an expert on this subject.'
4. 'Why are you wearing a sack?'
5. 'Of course you can do it. Why are we having this conversation?'
6. 'You look amazing!'
7. 'Obsessing isn't helping.'
8. 'Would you let me be treated the way you are letting him treat you?'
9. 'Just go, you'll have fun.'
10. 'I'm going to repeat what you just said back to you to see if you can hear how crazy you sound.'

DON'T LISTEN

1. 'OK, here's what he's thinking …'
2. 'Just buy it, it'll make you feel better.'
3. 'Send the email, it'll make you feel better.'
4. 'Have you checked your horoscope today?'
5. 'He'll DEFINITELY come crawling back by the end of the week.'
6. 'OK, here's what you have to do/say/wear when you meet up with him.'
7. 'Listen, there's only one way to have a real birth experience and that's at home, in front of an open fire, in a birthing pool, surrounded by love.'
8. 'Listen, there's only one way to have a safe birth experience and that's in a hospital, totally sanitised, doped up to the max, surrounded by doctors.'
9. 'I think we're getting too old for this.'
10. 'So I read this story in the *Daily Mail* …'

Ten signs you are having a non-awesome date (possibly autobiographical)

★ The date ends so early you stop off in Topshop on your way home, slightly drunk and buy a dress.

★ As you walk into the restaurant for this first date his face falls. 'Oh,' he says. 'I thought you were the other one.'

★ 'I don't mean to sound racist but …'

★ Somewhere in between the first and second course it transpires that he once slept with your sister.

★ You turn up, as primped and preened as a shih tzu at Crufts only to realise he not only saw this as just a friendly coffee but brought his girlfriend along to boot.

★ 'I know we just met but I just want to be honest so I'm going to say straight off the bat – I have herpes.'

* He starts crying halfway through and you find yourself reassuring him that you're sure he'll get back together with his ex-girlfriend as they're obviously meant to be together (yes, just like Steve Guttenberg does at the beginning of *Three Men and a Baby* – exactly that. You ARE Steve Guttenberg).
* 'You want to go home now? Man, Jews always leave early, don't you?'
* You have to wash your face when you get home because it is sticky with his slobbery saliva from when he licked your face. Literally, licked your face.
* 'You're how old and you're still single? Tick tock tick tock!'

Ten awesome women (in no particular order)

'There's no excuse for the young people not knowing who the heroes and heroines are or were' **Nina Simone, heroine**

Betty White

These days, Betty White is mainly known for two things: 1. being old and 2. being funny about it. But there is so much more to White than geriatric self-mockery. Aside from her brilliant performances on *The Golden Girls* and *The Mary Tyler Moore Show*, White was one of the first women to take control of her own acting career by co-founding a TV production company in the 1950s and making programmes for herself. She was also nominated for the first ever Best Actress Emmy in 1950 and her book about this period of her life, *Here We Go Again: My Life in Television*, is as funny as it is inspirational. Since her much beloved third husband, Allen Ludden, died in 1981, White has channelled the energies left over from her still ongoing acting career into animal rights, donating in one month alone $100,000 to the Los Angeles Zoo.

But she is no animal-centric, Bridget Bardot-like recluse. Still sharp as a tack in her tenth decade, she is not only a hilarious actress but a hysterical off-the-cuff guest on American talk shows, always happy to share her political views.

'That is one crazy bitch,' our Betty mused about Sarah Palin on the *Late, Late Show* with Craig Ferguson in 2008, casually swinging her pastel pantsuited legs about. Now, it is never nice to say such words about anyone but, in the case of Palin, I think White gets a free pass. And for the record, no one can rock a pastel pantsuit like Betty can.

Decca Mitford

In a highly competitive field, Decca has always struck me as the most extraordinary of the Mitford sisters. In a somewhat less competitive field, she is also the most admirable. The second youngest of the siblings, even as a child Decca renounced the very thing that partly, at the very least, still entrances so many people today about her family: their world of privilege. She saved up pennies throughout her childhood (just as her fictional alter ego, Jassy, does in *The Pursuit of Love*, written by Mitford's oldest sister Nancy) so as to be able to run away from home as soon as possible. Which, age nineteen, she did, with her even more militantly socialist cousin Esmond Romilly and the two lived in Spain, London and then America, passionately in love with one another.

Rejecting the right-wing and fascist politics of her class in general and her family in particular, Mitford became a lifelong socialist and, for some time, a member of the Communist Party in America, right in the thick of the McCarthy era.

After Romilly died in the Second World War, she married an American chap with the delightfully prosaic name of Bob Treuhaft. Together, they vigorously and courageously fought for civil rights and social justice in America and Mitford became an acclaimed investigative journalist. Her book, *The American Way of Death*, might not have the sparkle of her sister Nancy's novels but Decca was never interested in sparkle: instead, she wrote a sober, groundbreaking and still relevant study on, of all things, the funeral industry. You can't get less sparkly than that.

It is hard to think of a better example of nature triumphing over nurture than Decca Mitford. She lived the way she longed to, carving a path out of one unique life and into another.

Yet despite her vociferous disgust for the fascist politics of her sisters Unity, Diana and, for a brief spell, Nancy, she never stopped loving them and exchanged fond correspondence with them, as is right. Principles and morality were Mitford's bywords but she never denied where she came from and she always knew she was, in the purest sense, a Mitford sister.

Miss Piggy

Here is a woman – well, sow, really – who has a true sense of her self-worth. Despite being a TV and movie star, she has no self-defeating body insecurities or, for that matter, any insecurities whatsoever. She is damn good at what she does and she will be the first to tell you so. She is a strong, independent female yet one who is not afraid to be vulnerable and to show that she has needs, fearlessly laying herself open to rejection again and again as she proclaims her love for her 'Kermee'. The idea that self-deprecation or modesty are necessary qualities in an attractive female is as anathema to her as a bacon sandwich, and yet she does not shun femininity; it's just that, with her, 'femininity' means enjoying one's beauty and talents and taking it for granted that everyone else enjoys them too. She is Miss Piggy, and there is none more awesome.

Katharine Graham

Some people – heck, most people would have serious qualms about becoming the publisher of a major national newspaper, especially when they have had next to no experience and there are no other people of their gender in a similar position. Almost everyone, surely, would prefer to live out their days in peaceful equanimity if they had recently come through a heartbreakingly difficult marriage during which their spouse suffered from alcoholism and psychiatric problems and had recently killed himself. Buy a nice quiet house somewhere and spend their days having quiet lunches with friends and snoozing in the garden – that is what most people would prefer to do, seeking calm after such emotional upheavals. That is not what Katharine Graham did.

After her husband, Philip, committed suicide in 1963 she stepped in and, despite some initial difficulties with her male journalist colleagues who couldn't take a female colleague – let alone a boss – seriously, she took over his position as the publisher of the *Washington Post*.

And that was just the start. Graham helmed the *Washington Post* through its most exciting, high-profile and risky period, when it exposed the Watergate scandal, standing unwaveringly behind the reporters who uncovered it, Carl Bernstein and Bob Woodward, and the paper's editor, Ben Bradlee.

In her clear-sighted and unsentimental Pulitzer Prize-winning autobiography, *Personal History*, Graham writes excellently about the events of that time but the real story of the book is how a woman whose confidence had been destroyed when her beloved husband became abusive built herself back up again by finding her purpose in work and becoming, in turn, a legendary figure in American journalism.

Bea Arthur

Arthur was the star of two of the most radical sitcoms of all time, and it is an indictment of how so many social attitudes have gone backwards in America in the past few decades that neither of these programmes could be made now. As the eponymous Maude in the 1970s TV show Arthur played a liberal feminist married woman who, in one two-part episode, became the first woman on prime-time television to have an abortion (and two months before Roe v Wade, when abortion was legalised nationwide) because she and her husband simply don't want to have a baby. These days, American movies – never mind mainstream TV shows – can't even say the word abortion. In *The Golden Girls* (which was such an awesome show that it starred two of the most awesome women of all time) Arthur, along with her fabulous three co-stars, played Floridian pensioners who have fun, have issues and, most of all, have sex. I can't remember the last time I saw someone on American TV over the age of thirty having sex.

Arthur was also a great friend to Rock Hudson when many others abandoned him out of homophobia and, if you want to see the definition of awesomeness, look up on the internet the video of the two friends singing a duet about how dull drugs are. When someone once told Arthur that her height and deep voice made her a favourite among drag queens she replied, 'I'm flattered.' Bea Arthur was awesome.

Katharine Hepburn

The human embodiment of the word 'glorious', Hepburn defied every social convention at the time, for women, for stars and for human beings. She always wore trousers, she refused to play the ridiculous publicity games that the studios encouraged, she was a lifelong atheist and, having divorced her only husband after a youthful marriage, she vowed never to marry again despite plenty of offers, and instead spent her life secretly devoted to a married man, Spencer Tracy. Elizabeth Taylor and Richard Burton are generally described as the great twentieth-century love story but, to me, it's always been Hepburn and Tracy, her sharp edges softening whenever he would come into the room, according to onlookers, a love as tangible as silk.

But without him, and after him, Hepburn was as defiant in her dotage as she had been in her youth. When she was eighty-five Warren Beatty and Annette Bening came to dinner at hers, along with her friend and biographer, A. Scott Berg, who recorded the tale in his book about her, *Kate Remembered*. After learning, to her astonishment, that Bening and Beatty are married, Hepburn mutters to Berg, 'Poor girl.' When Berg replies that they seem very in love Hepburn, 'without missing a beat', replies, 'With the same man.'

She marched for woman's equality, supported Planned Parenthood and spoke out against McCarthyism at a time when such an act was near career suicide.

Hepburn lived life with her chin jutted proudly upwards, defiant, uncompromising and courageous.

Nina Simone

Oh, she was a pistol, was the woman born Eunice Kathleen Waymon. Belligerent, temperamental to the point that she was later diagnosed as bipolar, a notoriously unpredictable live performer and when asked in a 1999 interview whether the rumour about her pulling a gun on a record company boss who refused to pay her royalties was true, she replied, 'I sure damn did!' 'You actually pulled the trigger?' asked the astonished reporter. 'Fucking right I did,' was the unabashed reply. 'Sorry I didn't get him!' The reporter pointed out that 'men are going to be a bit nervous of you' to Simone. She didn't even let him finish the question: 'They are, very. But I refuse to cook or to clean. They've got to take me as I am and recognise that I'm a star as well as a woman and they have to deal with the two.'

Many think that much of Simone's anger had its roots in professional frustration. Despite her enormous success (although due to a combination of poor business judgement, tax difficulties and – this ol' story – a husband-cum-manager who stole from her, she only enjoyed a fraction of the financial rewards), Simone had actually wanted to be a classical musician and studied at the Julliard School of Music in New York. But in 1950s America, the easiest and maybe even the only path open to a young black woman who wanted to make her living out of music was the one marked blues and jazz, and so that is what Simone took.

This was perhaps the one time Simone compromised. She refused to be held back or confined by her race or gender and her music crossed the divides of both. In her wonderful autobiography, *I Put a Spell on You: The Autobiography of Nina Simone*, she emphasises that taking a stand is not just the business of men: 'It was always Marx, Lenin and revolution – real girls' talk.'

She was a passionate, even militant civil rights activist and her music became the soundtrack of the movement. She was utterly fearless in her defiance, introducing her song, 'Mississippi Goddamn' about the murder of Medgar Evers, with the proclamation, 'And I mean every word of it.' As if there could be any doubt.

Gloria Steinem

There are dozens and dozens of reasons to admire Gloria Steinem: the face of women's rights and the pro-choice movement for half a century, Steinem testified in the Senate on behalf of the Equal Rights Amendment, co-founded the Women's Action Alliance and remains, now well into her seventies, a tireless and deeply engaged campaigner on behalf of women's rights. Unlike her contemporary Betty Friedan, Steinem is a big supporter of gay rights and equality; unlike Germaine Greer, she has never appeared on a reality TV programme alongside the ex-wife of Sylvester Stallone. Steinem, thankfully, has no time for the tedious academic theorising that bogs down so much feminist discourse but favours instead plain speaking, good humour and common sense, avoiding the backbiting and sniping of which Greer is so embarrassingly fond. In response to the critics who yelped when Steinem, at the age of sixty-six, married environmentalist David Bale, she pointed out, quite rightly, that the institution of marriage had changed enormously since the days when she spoke against it in the 1970s. And anyway, she loved him and wanted to be with him and that was that. Bale then travelled around the country with her while she gave speeches, proving the model of a modern husband before his tragic death only three years after they married. Steinem is indefatigable and inspirational.

Hadley Richardson

My namesake and – perhaps more famously – Ernest Hemingway's first wife, therefore the only one who married him when he was unknown and humble as opposed to famous and arrogant.

Richardson was, by all accounts, quiet and kind, and recorded interviews reveal her to have had a cheeky sense of humour and a warm and ready laugh. She was also, judging from the photos of her, fond of culottes, and I approve of that.

The young couple moved to Paris and, unlike her starstruck husband, she was unimpressed by the famous people they met there – the Fitzgeralds, Gertrude Stein, Gerald and Sara Murphy – and these fame-dazzled narcissists were similarly not taken with her, dismissing her as dull and unworthy. Under the guidance of his tedious friends, though one suspects he didn't need much encouragement, Hemingway ditched his young wife and son at the first lick of a literary triumph.

But it was Richardson who had the better life – and certainly a happier one than any in the Parisian circle – enjoying a very contented marriage with the first winner of the Pulitzer Prize, and she lived well into her eighties.

Hemingway realised his mistake too late, writing of Richardson in *A Movable Feast*: 'I wished I had died before I loved anyone but her.'

Richardson was unencumbered with any such regrets. When a journalist later asked if she missed her famous friends and glamorous Parisian life she replied simply, 'No. I think I wanted something real.'

George Eliot, aka Marian Evans

In all honesty, *Middlemarch* aside, it has taken me a while to come round to George Eliot's novels. This is probably because I made the egregious error of starting with *Daniel Deronda*, her last novel and, by some measure, her dreariest. But even in the deadest midst of *Deronda*, when he's making yet another bloody speech about Zionism, I knew I liked George Eliot. I spent more time studying the completely fascinating portrait of Eliot on the back of the book than I did reading the wretched thing and no surprise: that thoughtful face, so endearingly plain with just a hint of a smile, gave a hint of her true nature. Namely, that Eliot was one of the sauciest and smartest women in the nineteenth century.

To the sauce first. Eliot fell in love with the married critic, George Henry Lewes, when she was thirty-two, a hopeless spinster by the standards of the day. For the rest of Lewes's life, the two of them openly had a relationship while he stayed married to his wife, and Eliot dedicated *The Mill on the Floss* to 'my beloved husband, George Henry Lewes'. Four years after Lewes died, Evans, at the age of sixty, managed to embark on a relationship even more scandalous than the previous one when she married John Cross, a chap who was twenty years younger than herself. When she died the following year, Cross wrote a somewhat sickeningly adoring biography of his wife.

As for the smarts, Eliot was brilliant. Aside from her novels, all of which engaged in political issues of the day, she did translations, wrote philosophical essays and reviews. She famously distanced herself from the usual types of novels written by women in her day in her essay, 'Silly Novels by Lady Novelists' and did so even more by taking on a male pseudonym, such was her determination to be taken seriously. She was a woman who refused to be bound by the conventions of the day, doing the work she wanted and living with the men she wanted when few women could do either. She wrote novels for the mind and pursued love from the heart. That is a life well lived.

Five awesome films and five very un-awesome films

AWESOME

Annie Hall

It is deeply sophomoric to let one's judgement of a piece of art be influenced by the real life story behind it but this is near impossible to avoid when it comes to certain Woody Allen films and, in particular, this film. After all, it's about a failed relationship between characters played by Allen and Diane Keaton, whose offscreen relationship had recently ended; many of the details are inspired by Keaton's actual life such as her anti-Semitic grandmother; Diane Hall is, in fact, Keaton's real name. So allowances in this case can be made.

Keaton remains Allen's most important muse. He wrote some wonderful roles for Mia Farrow (the superlative *The Purple Rose of Cairo*, the sublime *Radio Days*) but some of the Allen/Farrow films, no matter how wonderful, feel too weird, too sad to watch now, too weighted with retrospective knowledge of what was to come. This is particularly true in films that seem so prescient and awful in retrospect. *Husbands and Wives* is the prime example as it's about a couple splitting up which was mid-shoot when Farrow discovered Allen was having an affair with her adopted daughter, Soon-Yi Previn, and what a fun set that must have been to be on. But the glorious *Hannah and her Sisters* is equally difficult to watch nowadays. Farrow plays an offputtingly – in the eyes of her husband – perfect woman whose husband is having an affair with her sister. Meanwhile, a youthful Previn plays Farrow's daughter, romping about on camera while her adoptive father is sleeping with a member of his wife's family. In the harsh and unavoidable light of hindsight, *Hannah and her Sisters* looks about as creepy as *Manhattan*.

Annie Hall, by contrast, leaves nothing but a happy taste in the mouth, and the fact that it is so sweet despite being about an end of a relationship featuring two people who had actually broken up makes Allen's achievement even greater.

In *Woody Allen: A Documentary* by Robert Weide, Allen suggests that it was Keaton who broadened his perspective and *Annie Hall* did represent a major breakthrough for Allen whose films heretofore had featured none of the emotional honesty seen in *Annie Hall*. Moreover, the movie is extremely fair to the main female character, who is portrayed with real affection and sympathy and realism, not things one can really say about many of his later female characters. She is daffy but smart, desirable but not a slut: she is a human, not idealised, but ideal.

There is no bitterness when Annie ends the relationship, no simplification of someone being Good and someone being Bad (as there is in, say, *Midnight in Paris* in which Rachel McAdams's character is lazily rendered into an unfaithful bitch, meaning her fiancé, played by Owen Wilson, can happily pursue French ladies from all eras unencumbered by moral complications) – just an acknowledgement that sometimes two nice people can't make it work in the long run. True, Allen does cast (the short, plain, nebbishy) Paul Simon as the Hollywood bigshot for whom Annie leaves him when in real life Keaton jumped the Allen ship for (the tall, handsome and impossibly vain) Warren Beatty, and yes, the jibe might be immature. But it would take a more po-faced heart than mine not to applaud that cocked snoot.

The Philadelphia Story

It is a testament to how low the bar is for films in general including, I'm sorry to say, many Katharine Hepburn films in particular, that the fact Hepburn's character isn't 'tamed' by her male co-stars in this film marks *The Philadelphia Story* as really rather special. Rather, the message of this most wonderful of Hepburn films is that a true marriage should not involve a woman shrinking herself to fit in her conservative husband's little world, but should rather find a man who sees all that she could be, and loves her for it. If that man just happens to be Cary Grant, well, that's the glacé cherry on this chocolate cake of a movie.

Any film that features Hepburn, Grant and Jimmy Stewart is always going to be pretty damn great but *The Philadelphia Story*, far from coasting on its star power, is one of those rare movies that makes one – to quote, of all people, Dustin Hoffman in *Tootsie* – 'very proud of being a woman'. Unlike in, say, *Woman of the Year* and *Adam's Rib*, it is precisely Tracy Lord's (Hepburn) independence and outspokenness – qualities that Hepburn's performances always radiated – that make the good men in this film (Grant and Stewart) fall in love with her; it is the bad man – her fiancé, George Kittredge (John Howard) – who wants to do what her male co-stars and the studio heads in general repeatedly tried to do to Hepburn throughout her career: dull her edges.

Tracy might be spoilt, and she might have – momentarily – hidden her full-blooded individuality beneath the mask of 'a distant queen', but she is never dumb. In fact, she says one of the smartest lines said by anyone in any film, ever: 'The time to make up your mind about people,' Hepburn tells Grant at one point, looking especially glorious, 'is never.'

No one is straightforward and nothing is simple or simplistic in this film. Did I mention it was made in 1940? Truly, to use a very Hepburn word, this film is yar.

Say Anything

Yes, yes, John Cusack with the boombox, he gave her his heart, she gave him a pen: the greatest hits of *Say Anything* are well known. But what really raises this film up above the pantheon of great, great teen movies of the eighties for me is not Cusack's trench coat, Ione Skye playing a school nerd, Frasier's dad hiding in the bath when he's about to be arrested or even Peter Gabriel's still brilliant theme song – it's Cusack's endearing and totally believable relationship with his female friends, DC and particularly Corey played by the always wonderful and too little seen Lili Taylor.

This movie refutes *When Harry Met Sally*'s contention that men and women can't be friends: DC and Corey adore Lloyd Dobler (Cusack), can see his charms, want to protect him and also cheer him onwards – but they absolutely do not and never will fancy him, and this is something you almost never see in movies. In *Pretty in Pink*, for example, the central friendship between Duckie (Jon Cryer) and the truly great

Andy (Molly Ringwald – OBVIOUSLY) is underpinned and momentarily undone by his romantic feelings for her.

I mentioned the Bechdel Test in a previous chapter which ascertains if a movie treats women like more than love interests by posing the questions:

* Is there more than one woman in this film?
* Do they have names?
* Do they talk to one another about anything other than men?

That so many movies fail this test proves that movie executives believe that women onscreen (and maybe offscreen too, for all I know) are there solely to be saved and to be shagged. They aren't, in other words, humans in their own right with actual inner lives. They are there to make the male star look good, and this is quite some message to send. This also proves that, contrary to those annual newspaper articles puffing the importance of female audiences, movies are, still, largely aimed at men.

Similarly, when so few movies feature genuinely platonic friendships, this sends the message that the only point of the sexes interacting is to have sex. Anything else is boring and/or impossible.

Say Anything simply sticks up its nose at that nonsense and the close and caring friendship between Lloyd and Corey is my favourite thing about this film. Well, that and Corey's songs about her ex-boyfriend.

Auntie Mame
This could just as easily have gone in the Ten Awesome Books list because the original novel, written by Patrick Dennis, on

which the film is based is, indeed, awesome. But, you see, it is the law that any list of awesome films must and shall include one featuring Rosalind Russell, so here it is.

This 1957 film version of the hugely popular book and play not only shows off Russell at her absolute finest but also immortalises one of the greatest female characters of the twentieth century. Mame is an independent, bohemian, intelligent and, most of all, indefatigably fun woman, truly the ideal friend of any gender. She is utterly baffled by people who live their lives according to convention, preferring to caper about the world having 'adventures', yet she is wholly unselfish and devoted to her friends and, most of all, her nephew. She juts her chin at racists and humiliates anti-Semites at a time when anti-Semitism was seen by some as simple good sense. When she loses all her money in the stock market crash, this former upper-class woman gamely works in a series of menial jobs; when her husband dies on their honeymoon, she distracts herself writing her autobiography which becomes a bestseller.

It's strange that Mame is not cited more often in lists of top female film characters because, really, if the sight of Russell striding about a New York apartment in a crystal-studded pantsuit, smoking a cigarette in an ivory holder, defending the rights of single mothers and outsmarting an awful socialite with her wit and magic floating furniture isn't the very definition of feminism, I'll eat my bra.

But even aside from all that, this movie is pure pleasure, sweet, inspiring and hilarious, nutritious as well as delicious, the very thing to watch on a rainy Sunday afternoon.

(Sort of) interesting film trivia! The boring story that Patrick's awful fiancée Gloria tells Mame about the ping pong game she played with Bunny Bixler in which 'I stepped on the ball' is referenced in *Trading Places* in the country club scene when one of the snobby girlfriends laughs about someone who 'stepped on the ball'. How about that for film history?

Rushmore

This film is generally remembered for Bill Murray's wonderful performance, Jason Schwartzman's Marmite-like quirky one and the establishment of Wes Anderson's distinctive aesthetic. Yet it also features two of the finest and unfairly overlooked female characters of recent years, Miss Cross (a brilliant Olivia Williams) and Margaret Yang (Sara Tanaka), a non-cartoon version of Lisa Simpson if ever there was one, and that is a very high compliment indeed. These women refute the criticisms that are frequently lobbed at Anderson, namely, that he is an overly ironic, faintly sexless hipster, one more interested in aesthetics than actual human emotions. Miss Cross could easily have been just a two-dimensional, idealised character, a male fantasy or – almost worse – the stern woman who makes the immature men grow up (see: every Judd Apatow film). Instead, she is smart, sad, sexual, kind, confused, needy and strong. 'She's sweet, but she's fucked up,' is a heartbroken Herman Blume's (Murray) take and, really, who isn't?

Margaret Yang, icon to female nerds everywhere, has the confidence to go after Max (Schwartzman), even when he appears to rebuff her, the inner steel to tell him – quite roundly – that he is her boyfriend when he blushes at the title and the intelligence never to disguise her academic skills; but she is not perfect. Rather, she cheated on her prize-winning science project, something she owns up to quite readily when Max asks, because she never tries to impress him. She is simply, always, wonderfully, just her own honest self. As an extra treat, the film's last scene is soundtracked by and ironises 'Ooh La La' by the Faces, one of the catchiest and most bitterly anti-female songs in the pantheon, underlying the foolishness of Max and Herman to idealise women who are, as they learn, only human like themselves.

Incidentally, Anderson also created another of my favourite female characters, Margot Tenenbaum, in his next film, *The Royal Tenenbaums*. That his following two films, *The Life Aquatic* with Steve Zissou and, most of all, *The Darjeeling Limited*, featured such absolutely dreadful female roles seems only more disappointing by comparison.

NON-AWESOME

The Sex and the City films

Oh my Lord, where to begin? The way both of these movies betrayed the message of the TV show (or, at least, the first three series of it) that women can and do lead satisfying lives unshackled by marriage? That they betray the female fans of the show by suggesting all western women are body-obsessed, label-obsessed, ring-obsessed morons? That they betray anyone with a brain with dialogue, plot lines, and scenarios that make you feel you are being lobotomised with a pink teaspoon? Yes, yes, yes, all that and so much more.

These films are terrible in and of themselves, no question. But it is the way they sell out the loyal fans of the long-running TV show, and suggest that Sarah Jessica Parker and Michael Patrick King became so blinded by their television success and crippled with panic in the face of transferring it to the big screen that they lost sight of the show's original

USP (namely, that it featured smart dialogue in the mouths of interesting, clever and independent women) that puts these films in this list as opposed to being simply dismissed as more examples of female-hating movies for women (see: every single Katherine Heigl film ever made).

These movies are unwatchably awful and they destroyed the once ace *Sex and the City* franchise. Bravo, everyone. Bravo.

Love, Actually

This film is so shockingly bad that it would border on misogyny if it wasn't clearly just stupid as opposed to malicious.

Two of the women held up in the film as being particularly desirable are domestic staff, working for the men they attract. Because nothing's sexier than a woman who cleans and serves tea to you – amirite or amirite?! In one of those cases, the woman isn't even able to speak English, just to up the inequality in that relationship, to say nothing of the implausibility. Aside from the couple who meet acting on a porn film set, the one relationship in which a woman is in some way the professional equal of the man she likes is scuppered because the woman (the reliably luminous Laura Linney) deigns to have some kind of familial responsibility, which obviously renders her incapable of being loved. If you're gonna be with a man, Laura, then you have to be able to give him 100 per cent attention.

Look, I don't actually think Richard Curtis is some evil woman-hater. But I do think he made a sloppily terrible film in which a lot of screwy messages slipped in without his noticing. Don't see this movie. It is most non-awesome.

Pretty Woman

It doesn't matter how fun that shopping scene is, or how great the Roxette song still sounds: this movie is one of the weirdest films ever made, the kind that makes you wonder not just how it was such a success, but how it got green-lit in the first place. It's not the message that being a prostitute is kinda sexy and cool and you'll look as healthy as Julia Roberts and end up with a handsome rich man that bugs me (although that's not great). I get that the film isn't saying this happens to every prostitute. Yes, I do get that. Rather, it's the intimation that getting together with a man who picks up hookers is any kind of happily ever after for anyone that gets my goat. Congratulations, lady! You're marrying a man who pays for blow jobs – every little girl's dream! Interesting fact: *Pretty Woman* came out just the year before *Thelma and Louise*, and yet which film has proven to have the longer afterlife? Well, when was the last time you saw *Thelma and Louise*? The dread pirate Roberts was right: life is pain.

Funny Face

Based not just on a play but loosely on the real-life relationship between photographer Richard Avedon and the model Doe Nowell Avedon, *Funny Face* is one of those films – like *Belle de Jour* and *Love Story* – that is remembered fondly today, yet more for the wardrobe than the film itself. And rightly so, because Hepburn's outfits are, as usual, gorgeous but the film? Not so much. Hepburn's character, Jo Stockton, is repeatedly mocked, by both the characters and the film for her literary curiosity and interest in anything that isn't fashion. Happiness, the message of the movie seems to be, can only come to a woman when she stops trying to educate herself, puts on a pretty frock and smiles for the camera.

Look, I don't like to knock any film that stars Fred Astaire, plus I always enjoy any 1950s film that features a token fashion show (see also: *How to Marry a Millionaire*, *Singin' in the Rain*). But let's be frank here: this film is ridiculous.

The Devil Wears Prada

While ostensibly being a women's film about women who work, *The Devil Wears Prada* shows a remarkable keenness to punish working women. Both Miranda (Meryl Streep) and Andrea (Anne Hathaway) are left by their partners because they dare to be late occasionally to dinner due to their high-pressured jobs and Andrea is only reunited with her boyfriend when she bows to his wish that she quit her job. This, incidentally, is presented as a happy ending.

The movie thinks it can get away with this laughably retrograde stance because fashion, it is generally accepted, is silly. Thus, to take a job in the fashion industry seriously – more seriously than a relationship – is, the movie insinuates, misguided. Even *Sex and the City*, a TV show that was far more about fashion than either of the topics in its title, fell victim to this when it introduced a *Vogue* editor, played by Candice Bergen. This woman may have been successful, but the trade-off was that she had no social life and the best she could hope for was sharing a boyfriend with a younger woman.

Besides the unacceptable idea of women working, there is the added crime that they work in an industry run by other women. Hence, fashion journalists in movies are depicted as childish, sniping about one another's weight and clothes. Because that's what happens when women work together, you know – if they weren't so underweight that they'd stopped menstruating, they'd throw tampons at one another. I have yet to see a movie or TV show set in a fashion magazine in which the heroine is not urged to seek out the one man in the office for any crumbs of kindness or intelligence, as happens in *The Devil Wears Prada*, continuing to tick off the clichés. Sure, he's probably gay, but at least he's not all oestrogen.

That the book on which this film was based caused such a stir when it was published in 2003 is yet another example of this sexist attitude to the fashion industry. Certainly if the personal assistant of the editor of, say, *GQ* or *Esquire* had published a book it wouldn't have garnered such, if any, attention. But that is because the media are not half as fascinated with the editors of men's magazines as they are with Wintour. But as someone who used to cover men's fashion shows and spent several weeks on the road with editors of men's magazines, those dudes are no slouch when it comes to pernicketiness, egotism and bossiness and can rival Wintour in any of those areas. In other words, they behave like ambitious people who have had to fight hard to get to the top of a very competitive industry. But, hey, they're men so that's the norm. A woman who is like that must be a freak and, thus, she must be mocked, pilloried and punished until she quits her job and behaves in a more acceptably feminine manner. Right?

Ten awesome books

Persuasion, by Jane Austen

Pride and Prejudice is good, sure, but *Persuasion* is the Austen connoisseur's choice. It is Austen's last completed novel and it has the smack of wisdom and peace attained from middle age, albeit interspersed with Austenishly caustic digs at her hated town of Bath. Anne Elliot, a spinster at twenty-seven, is the Austen heroine I root for more than any other, quiet and sad, yes, but also wise and secretly sharp. The other families, especially the Musgroves, are wonderfully silly in that Austen way, but also sympathetically drawn, and Captain Wentworth is, to my eyes, the best of Austen's leading men, neither sulky, damaged nor overly posh – just a smart, sensitive man whose heart had been badly broken. Most of all, the message of the book is that a woman should never take advice from anyone about how to conduct her romantic life but should rather trust herself, a moral that can never be said too often.

American Wife, by Curtis Sittenfeld

I've already mentioned Sittenfeld's other two wonderful novels – *Prep* and *The Man of my Dreams* – in previous chapters so let's now chuck in the third for the hat trick. This is an amazing portrait of an ordinary woman in an extraordinary marriage, and is particularly excellent on the nuances of the female protagonist's psyche: her childish shyness, her teenage guilt, her adult sexual desire, her marital contentment born out of the compromises any long-term relationship – but especially this long-term relationship – requires. Only Sittenfeld could have made Laura Bush an every woman. She is, by some distance, one of the finest writers working today.

Eloise, by Kay Thompson and Hilary Knight

At the risk of infantilising myself, if I could be any character from any work of fiction in the world, I would choose to be Eloise. Spending my days scampering about the Plaza Hotel in New York, hair all askew, lolling about with my pug Weenie and my turtle Skipperdee, pestering the bell captain and skating up and down the hallways to annoy the other hotel guests and avoid my maths tutor – who can honestly say that this does not sound like true metropolitan heaven? Happily, this life of flipping Riley is not wasted on the undeserving: Eloise is the little girl I wish I had been – smart, sassy, endlessly imaginative and unhindered by shyness of any kind, patrolling the Plaza as if it were her kingdom, which, indeed, it is. The finest of children's books featuring the finest of children.

A Girl's Guide to Fishing and Hunting, by Melissa Bank

The only problem with this delicious book about, mainly, a young woman's progress from teenage years to adulthood is that it will make you regret that you are not the best friend of the author, Melissa Bank, whose voice is so wise and warm and witty that it feels an absolute crime not to know her personally. Still, at least we have her books, this and its bafflingly underrated follow-up, *The Wonder Spot*, in her stead. *A Girl's Guide* is constructed as a series of essays, each one (with the exception of one about her neighbour) describing a certain episode in the life of Jane, from the time her older brother brought home a girlfriend to her bout with breast cancer to her relationship with a much older man. But the real strengths of this book are its appealing tone, smart details and tender humour that refute any accusations of it being just another piece of chick lit. The last essay, incidentally, about the time Jane tries to follow the advice in a dating book that bears more than a passing similarity to *The Rules* has the same message of *Persuasion*, which, I repeat, cannot be said too often.

The Collected Dorothy Parker

Like her British counterpart and contemporary, Nancy Mitford, what Parker lacked in personal contentment, she made up for in brilliance, wit and writing that is often heavily tinged with the bittersweet. Her short stories, particularly those about relations between the sexes, are wise enough to stop them from tipping over into bitterness ('Big Blonde' is probably the best known example), while her timelessly quotable poems and lyrics pack far more emotion than their jaunty tone suggests. Yet it's her journalism that I love the most, especially her Constant Reader column for the *New Yorker* and her book reviews for *Esquire*. Parker's tone makes her sound as palpably present as if she were chatting with you on your sofa, as opposed to writing over a half a century ago, and her observations are still as pertinent (she's damn right: Holly Golightly does sound 'a truly awful pest'). She is one of those rare writers whose opinion you want to know about everything because whatever she says, it is always interesting. I wouldn't advise reading this book all in one go because Parker's vibrancy combined with sadness make for a dizzying immersive effect when taken in large doses. But for dipping in and out, there is none better.

Franny and Zooey, by J.D. Salinger

Salinger is generally thought of as a boys' author, or, more specifically, the disaffected boys' author, one for sulky teenagers, the real life Donny Darkos of the world. But this is only because the distracting success of *The Catcher in the Rye* overshadowed the rest of his writing, writing that is far more tender and empathetic than one might expect from the man most people think of as the voice of Holden Caulfield.

The Glass family is my favourite of Salinger's creation, the story of seven uptown New York siblings who were child prodigies and are now stumbling through life as adults, all too smart for their own good. The Glasses recur throughout Salinger's work, including the short story, 'A Perfect Day for Bananafish', the heartbreaking novel *Raise High the Roof Beam, Carpenters* and *Seymour: An Introduction* and *Franny and Zooey*, the novel about the youngest siblings.

The first half, 'Franny', tells the seemingly simple story about the eponymous young student visiting her awful boyfriend, Lane, at what is suggested to be Princeton. Salinger captures wonderfully Franny's swift meltdown, unconfident in herself despite being much smarter than Lane, attempting to be girlishly polite to him while at the same time losing interest in his petty concerns. Whenever I catch myself feigning interest to a man who is banging on about his achievements, Franny comes to mind. In the second half, the extremely close and grief-tinged relationship between Franny and her brother Zooey is depicted with real fondness and sweetness. A lovely book and one that will make you want to go beyond *Catcher* on the Salinger shelf.

My Fat, Mad Teenage Diary, by Rae Earl

Oh Lordy, I love this book. It has been described, inevitably, as Adrian Mole's sister's diary, and that is both accurate and, in my opinion, a very good thing. It is the actual teenage diary of the writer and broadcaster Rae Earl, who has, thankfully, allowed the rest of the world to read it, and nod with recognition. Set in 1989, it is the story of the boy-crazy, Morrissey-obsessed, overweight teenager Rae, who takes herself incredibly seriously, which makes her writing even funnier than when she is deliberately being funny – which she is, often. No description will convey how brilliant this book is so just trust me, this book is hilarious – an English comedy classic, really.

The Pursuit of Love, by Nancy Mitford

It mystifies me that some critics – and they are numerous – take such umbrage with Nancy Mitford's writing, reducing it to nothing more than shallow japes and general callowness. According to one, it displays 'an attitude to life forged in that artificial late-Twenties crucible in whom the events of a decade later can only raise a kind of forced inanity'.* To another, Mitford's writing exemplifies a 'posh aesthetic'

---

* *Bright Young People*, D.J. Taylor.

which 'appeals to people who want life's profundities to scatter on the wind like a handful of confetti … For the devoted toff, effort and compassion are embarrassing in life and horrific on the page.'*

I can only assume that these critics have never read *The Pursuit of Love*, Mitford's breakthrough literary success. Yes, the larks and screams of laughter that her critics find so off-putting do feature in the novel, mainly in her early descriptions of the Redesdale family, a thinly disguised depiction of Mitford's own family. But only the most obtuse reader could fail to hear, beneath the japes, the pain, sorrow and, yes, compassion that underscore this novel, the catch in the throat telling the joke.

This comes mainly from the story of the Parisian love affair between the novel's heroine, Linda Radlett, and Fabrice de Sauveterre, an even more thinly disguised version of Gaston Palewski, French politician and the love of Mitford's life. She cleverly contrasts this affair with the marriage of Fanny, Linda's cousin and the novel's narrator, who weds early, safely and somewhat boringly, unlike Linda who forsakes security for moments of head-spinning passion. This question about which is preferable as a romantic life – safety but boredom versus excitement but uncertainty – feels as relevant today, for men and women, as it did in Mitford's time, perhaps even more so now that men and women have more choice.

Even in fiction, and even though she wrote *Pursuit* in the very early days of her affair with Palewski, Mitford, clear-eyed about herself to a fault, could only envisage an unhappy ending for 'Fabrice' and 'Linda'. And she was right, there was

---

* Andrew O'Hagan, *London Review of Books*, 15 November 2007.

no happily ever after for Mitford and Palewski (although, poignantly, Mitford does give their fictional versions a baby when she herself could not have children). But her deep love for him, as well as her humour, intelligence and unblinking courage live for ever in her testament of her love for him in this, a compassionate and profound treat of a novel.

Heartburn, by Nora Ephron

'Above all, be the heroine of your life, not the victim,' the journalist, essayist, novelist, screenwriter, film director, playwright, food connoisseur and all-round awesome lady, Nora Ephron, once said in one of her many deliciously brilliant quotes, and no book adheres to this instruction better than Ephron's own novel, *Heartburn*. Just as snappy, smart and timeless as Ephron's other great masterpiece, *When Harry Met Sally*, *Heartburn* is based on the disintegration of Ephron's glittering marriage to Carl Bernstein after he had an affair with – of all people – Margaret Jay when Ephron was pregnant with their second child. Both Bernstein and Ephron were high-profile writers, him because of his work in exposing the Watergate scandal and her because of her brilliantly funny journalism, not least her essays charting the 1970s feminist movement (collected in another awesome book, *Crazy Salad*, which is massively recommended), and so the collapse of their marriage in 1980 garnered a certain amount of attention. Ephron, however, refused to be the victim and, just two years later, published *Heartburn* which manages to be scathingly funny about her ex-husband – who she memorably describes as 'capable of having sex with a Venetian blind' – without being bitter, sympathetic without being pathetic and funny without being glib.

Heartburn is a brilliant book in its own right, inexhaustibly hilarious and piercingly wise, but considering that this golden joy was built out of such bitter ashes, it is downright miraculous.

Bridget Jones's Diary, by Helen Fielding

I know I've banged on about this novel quite a lot already, but that is because *Bridget Jones's Diary* is, quite simply, awesome. If I were only allowed to read three books for the rest of my life, *Bridget Jones's Diary* would absolutely be one of those books. Yes, it does adhere to the classic marriage ending which I have railed against so heartily elsewhere (as, for the record, does *Persuasion*). But – and I appreciate this is something of a maverick viewpoint – the whole Bridget/Darcy plot is, for me, such a minor part of the book. To me, the book's real strengths are the extraneous details that are completely inessential to the plot but essential to the novel's three-dimensional brilliance, things like Bridget's mother's insistence that getting one's colours done at Colour Me Beautiful is the answer to all ills; Bridget's attempts to ape Kenneth Tynan's dead wife's famed 'inner poise' ('Wish to be like Kathleen Tynan, though not, obviously, dead'); her friends who are all individualised and perfect, especially Tom and Magda; and, most of all, the tonally perfect and unforgettably quotable phrases such as 'terrifying slide into obesity – why? Why?'

In other words, it's Fielding's writing that makes this book so special and, for me, inspirational, if intimidatingly so. Every sentence is so casually but perfectly turned, every observation so spot-on. It is a rare day that I don't quote some line from Bridget Jones to someone or, more commonly, in my head (more times than I'd care to admit have I locked myself in a pub or office loo in a panic 'and sat down, staring crazily at the door with one eye').

I have read this book a thousand times and, if I'm lucky, I will read it at least a thousand more. I love this book.

Acknowledgements

Huge yet insufficient thanks to the following awesome people:

Nell Freeman Romilly, Carol Miller, Andy Bull, Imogen Fox, Tim Robey, Irin Carmon, Tim Lusher, Richard Williams, India Knight, Ed Howker, Simon Amstell, Charlie Angela and George Glass for the *Funny Face* reminder and much more, the Graff family for the Shakespeare lesson, Daniel Lee for his *Home and Away* expertise (apologies for being such a vulgar dame, Daniel), Lauren Collins, Georgia Garrett, Louise Haines, Georgia Mason.